IMAGES
of America

ALONG MANHASSET BAY

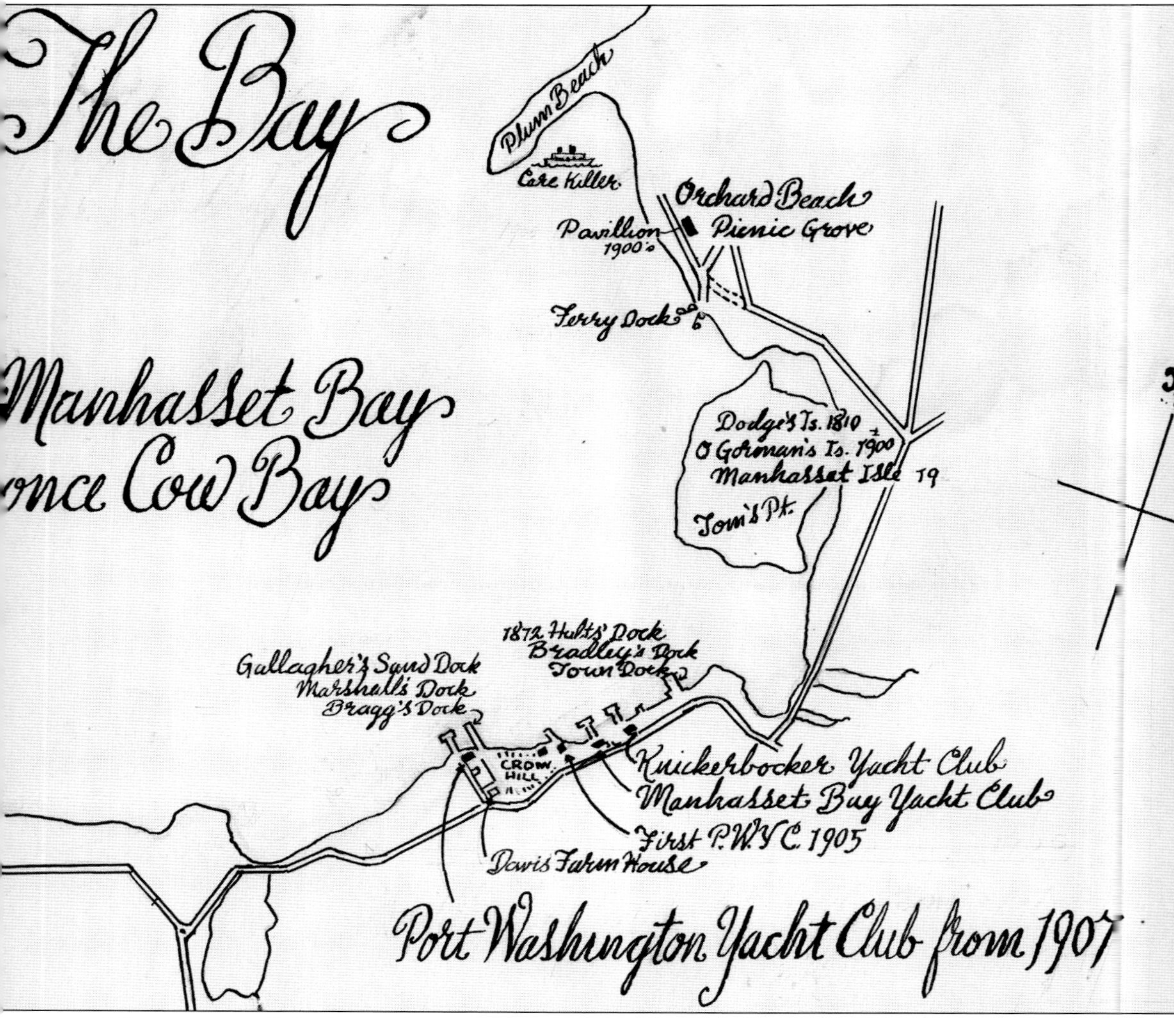

The naming of Manhasset Bay took place over 300 years. Its earliest names were Cow Bay and Sint Sink by the Matinecock tribe of Algonquin Indians who first inhabited the peninsula. Later names of European influence included Howe's Bay, Schouts Bay, and the lesser-known Muskite Bay (noted on a c. 1770s French map). Manhasset Bay would not be named as such until 1907. This hand-drawn map from 1907 uses that name, marking areas of interest, including the early assortment of yacht clubs that populated the shoreline. (Courtesy of the Port Washington Public Library.)

On the Cover: This photograph from 1900 is believed to show members of the Navin family along the Manhasset Bay shoreline in Port Washington. William Navin (1903–2000), not pictured, lived at 81 Ivy Way. A prominent patent attorney, he was a man of many interests. A writer, poet, and teacher of history and English at the Port Washington High School in the mid-1920s, he was also a contributing writer for the *Port Washington News*. Navin often wrote about matters relating to the Port Washington waterfront. (Courtesy of the Port Washington Public Library.

IMAGES
of America

ALONG MANHASSET BAY

Vanessa Nastro and
the Port Washington Public Library

ARCADIA
PUBLISHING

ISBN 978-1-4671-0502-6

Published by Arcadia Publishing
Charleston, South Carolina

Printed in the United States of America

Library of Congress Control Number: 2019957385

For all general information, please contact Arcadia Publishing:
Telephone 843-853-2070
Fax 843-853-0044
E-mail sales@arcadiapublishing.com
For customer service and orders:
Toll-Free 1-888-313-2665

Visit us on the Internet at www.arcadiapublishing.com

This book is dedicated to the memory of Virginia "Ginger" Marshall Martus, whose immense support of and contributions to the nautical and local history of Port Washington will forever be remembered.

This book is also dedicated to those who have encouraged and advanced the study of local history on Long Island. It also recognizes the efforts of individuals and organizations that have contributed to the acquisition and preservation of archival records for the benefit of the general public.

Contents

Acknowledgments

As with many local history collections, the Port Washington Public Library is indebted to its community members for supplying countless photographs over the years, several of which are presented in this publication. I would like to extend my sincerest gratitude to Andy Christensen, Bill and Priscilla Ciccariello, Alan Dinn, Barbara E. Fishman, Betty Gimbel, Alicia McCarvill, Rose Osterberg, R. John Pellaton, Victor Raimondo, and David Smith.

A very special thank-you goes to Jim Flemings and Donald and Warren White, who supplied us with immensely entertaining anecdotes and photographs of their first-hand experiences living and working along Manhasset Bay. Thank you to the Nautical Advisory Committee at the Port Washington Public Library for their continued support and contributions to our maritime heritage.

I would like to acknowledge the generous assistance of archivist Elly Shodell, volunteer Robert Bracken, and library trainee Elizabeth Rowland, who assisted with research both onsite and offsite, caption material, and proofreading of this publication. Thank you to William Salas at the Smithtown Public Library for patent research. Invaluable assistance was provided by local libraries in communities on Manhasset Bay: Christy Orquera at the Great Neck Public Library, Alice Kramer and Leila Mattson for their collective knowledge and expertise on the history of Great Neck, and images provided by the History Center at the Manhasset Public Library.

I would also like to thank the Village of Port Washington North for offering images and access to village records. Thank you to Port Washington North mayor Bob Weitzner, village clerk Palma Torrisi, and deputy clerk Linda Kropacek.

Special thanks go to our editor at Arcadia Publishing, Caroline Anderson, whose enthusiasm and patient guidance ensured smooth sailing and clear text.

Thank you to Regina Feeney at the Freeport Memorial Library for continued support, guidance, and friendship.

Thank you to Keith Klang, director of the Port Washington Public Library, and the board of trustees, for ongoing support for local history-related projects.

Unless otherwise noted, all images are courtesy of the Port Washington Public Library.

INTRODUCTION

The waters of Manhasset Bay have long been an incubator for livelihood and commerce, recreation, and industrial advancement. Forming the northeastern boundary of the Great Neck Peninsula and the southeastern boundary of Cow Neck (Port Washington Peninsula or Manhasset Neck), the bay is approximately 4.5 miles north to south and about a mile wide. Designated by New York State as a concentrated area of marine development as well as a coastal fish and wildlife habitat and labeled by the National Audubon Society as an important bird area, its present ecological significance recalls those important characteristics that attracted its earliest inhabitants over 400 years ago. Its well-stocked waters first attracted the Matinecock tribe of Algonquin Native Americans, who used the bay for fishing and shellfish harvesting. From the settlement of Cow Neck in the 1700s, the bay held opportunities for those seeking sustainability on the surrounding farmlands.

With the influx of 17th century Dutch and English settlers utilizing the bay and surrounding grazing pastures, farming and fishing became major industries. Through most of the 1800s, Manhasset Bay was recognized as the largest oystering harbor on the North Shore of Long Island, referred to as the "shellfish garden of New York City."

The 19th century brought great changes to the peninsula: the New York and Flushing Rail Road extended service to Great Neck in 1866, reaching Manhasset and Port Washington in 1898.

The shores of Manhasset Bay also gave way to other industry. Once known as the "Plymouth Rock" of American aviation history, Port Washington was a thriving hub of air and seaplane activity in the 1920s and 1930s. Nearly all of Manhasset Isle was once occupied by seaplane bases, airports, and hangars. Crowds would gather to witness launches from the bay. Aircraft based at the home of a fledgling Pan American Airways on Port Washington's Manhasset Isle set new records for speed and altitude above the waters of Manhasset Bay. Various planes were tested here by Charles Lindbergh and Glenn Curtiss as well.

Sailing craft were an integral part of Manhasset Bay's maritime history, both occupational and recreational. An encyclopedic variety of seafaring vessels plied the bay from the late 1800s to the 1940s—ferries, motorboats, yawls, barges, tugs, sloops, freighters, hydrofoils, flying boats, yachts, rowboats, scows, trawlers, iceboats, and steamers.

Around 1900, the shoreline flourished as a weekend destination for New York City residents looking for a summer respite from their work life. Excursion boats from Manhattan and the Bronx brought visitors to an area then known as Locust Grove in Port Washington. As the waters of Manhasset Bay brought industry to its shores, the harbor attracted a leisure crowd with yacht clubs, hotels, and restaurants dotting the shoreline. This attracted the attention of wealthy residents who would soon construct grand estates along the northern shores of Port Washington, Great Neck, and Plandome.

Sand mining in Port Washington took place from the 1860s through the 1980s. Between 1865 and 1930, one hundred million tons of sand was delivered to New York City to build skyscrapers, subways, and sidewalks. Many builders specified "Cow Bay sand" because of its excellent composition. The peninsula was changed by the influx of sand mining companies staking claims to large portions of land in Manorhaven, Port Washington North, and the Hempstead Harbor shoreline. While the sand mining industry brought prosperity and notoriety, its use of heavy machinery leveled the peninsula, once known for its tree-covered hilltops. Ambitious real estate developers planned expansive residential communities, publicizing the beauty of the Manhasset Bay shoreline and all it had to offer.

The history of Manhasset Bay is inextricably linked to its maritime heritage. While many of these traditions are no longer practiced, they are preserved by the testimonies of those who lived and worked on the bay and who seek to preserve its legacy.

Oral histories are the oldest form of historical information, predating the written word. This book was greatly influenced by the Port Washington Public Library's vast collection of oral histories, dating to 1976. Many of the captions directly quote selections from these testimonies, and their narratives inform many of the pages in this publication. An invaluable addition to the written and photographic record, oral history provides first-hand testimony by the people who were eyewitness to the events of the past. While researching this book, I conducted additional interviews and numerous site visits, which have reaffirmed my own commitment to preserving the history of Manhasset Bay and all it represents.

In 2017, the library received a generous gift from the estate of longtime Port Washington resident and maritime historian Virginia Marshall Martus. Not only was she a supporter of the library, she also helped found important local history programs and projects such as the maritime oral history collection. In honor of her important contributions, the library will continue to promote Long Island's maritime heritage through educational programming. Royalties from the sale of this book will also go toward programs and projects highlighting Long Island history.

One

Hospitality on the Bay

Gildo's Restaurant opened its doors on September 9, 1938. Owner Gildo Navone ran a refined and well-ordered establishment in Port Washington for nearly 30 years. Pictured is Gildo's executive chef (second from right) preparing for the dinner rush with his sous chef and assistant cooks around 1950.

Having gone through several adaptations since it first opened in 1890, the Renwick Hotel (now Diwan Restaurant) remains a landmark on the old Port Washington waterfront. Located on the corner of Shore Road and Mill Pond Road, the original structure was built by Lorenzo B. Smull, a partner in the contracting firm of Smull and Walsh, who also built Port Washington's first high school in 1908. The image above from the turn of the 20th century shows the grandeur of the building's original façade. The first-floor porch where guests could dine al fresco has since been enclosed, although the sizable balcony on the second floor is still there. The hotel was later named the Bayview Hotel and was operated by "Pop" Konrad. When Gildo Navone and Rico Cantino acquired the hotel in 1938, it was known as DeMar's.

An elegant buffet celebrated Gildo's opening night on September 9, 1938. Gildo Navone, an Italian immigrant, realized a long-held dream when he opened this restaurant on Shore Road with views of Manhasset Bay and Mill Pond. Prior to acquiring the former Renwick Hotel in 1938, Navone was for many years a steward at Port Washington's Knickerbocker Yacht Club. Opening night, a reservation-only event, attracted a well-heeled crowd, garnered extensive coverage in the local press with photographs from the studio of Stanley Gerard Mason, and captivated attendees with Navone's beautifully prepared Italian-French dishes that included blue point clams casino, supreme of grapefruit, cream of chicken a La Reine, roast stuffed Maryland turkey with chestnut dressing, perigourdine, salad Waldorf, crepe suzette, zabaglione, and friandise. Restaurateur Gildo Navone created something special that evening in 1938, and the refined cuisine developed a reputation beyond the Port Washington community, enabling it to remain a mainstay of restaurant-goers for more than 30 years.

The Port Washington Hotel was built in the 1870s by Peter Hults, opening on October 17, 187
Located right on Manhasset Bay at 346 Main Street, the hotel, pictured here around 1900, offere
guests sea breezes and beautiful views of the water. In 1905, John F. Bradley purchased the buildin
renaming it Bradley's Hotel. Later, the hotel no longer accommodated overnight guests, instea
becoming an upscale eatery called Bradley's Shore Restaurant. Bradley's, as it became know
was famous on Long Island, offering delectable seafood dishes to notable guests such as New Yor
City mayors Jimmy Walker and John Francis Hylan as well as prominent writers, performers, an
sports figures such as Jack Dempsey. It was also an important gathering place for members of th
Port Washington community, hosting dinner parties, clambakes, and dances that were the tal
of the town. Sadly, the building was destroyed by fire in the early 1960s.

Pigs were raised near Bradley's restaurant, and it was not uncommon for owner John Bradley to host a "hog guessing" or "hog killing." This advertisement from 1916 that Bradley extensively circulated would allow guests to guess the weight of the selected hog, which would then be killed, roasted, and served to dinner guests.

A common locale for community gatherings, Bradley's enclosed porch was the perfect location for large events such as this one from around 1920 photographed by Louis Bischoff. Favored not only for its ideal location along Manhasset Bay, its menu boasted an extensive selection of seafood dishes (sourced locally from the bay) as well as special menus for high-profile events. Diners could feast on gastronomic delights such as green turtle a l'Anglaise, Currituck mallard duck, and Arctic pudding au rhum, to name just a few.

Halsey House, or Halsey Hall, later known as the Rose Tree Inn, was a well-known boardinghouse on Manhasset Bay in Port Washington. Located at 378 Main Street, it was built by Lorenzo Smull, who also helped build the Renwick Hotel and the Main Street School, and was used as Smull's personal residence until his death in 1919. The home was then acquired by Elizabeth Halsey, who ran the Victorian-style mansion as a restaurant and boardinghouse until around 1930.

This postcard shows the Anchorage, probably around the late 1880s or 1890s. It was built in 177 by John Mitchell, whose family occupied the homestead for many years. Located on the corner c Main Street and Third Avenue, the "old Mitchell Homestead," as it was originally named, has bee remembered as the site of a robbery and murder that took place on May 13, 1773. Six whalebo men, under the cover of night, broke into the home and shot and killed John's son Benjami Mitchell. The property was renamed the Anchorage when the homestead was acquired by retire captain Elbert Stannard, an accomplished seaman who also leased much of the waterfront in Po Washington. After the captain's death in 1907, the building was used as a summer boardinghou referred to as the Haskell House. It was later demolished.

Originally a bayman, Adelbert Van Wicklen, son of Capt. William Van Wicklen, saw the money-making potential of the Manhasset Bay shoreline. A member of the Knickerbocker Yacht Club, Van Wicklen competed in the club's annual iceboat races, winning the title in 1908. He was a busy Port Washington entrepreneur who operated several businesses. One of his first was the small lobster house seen above around 1910. Van Wicklen's diverse endeavors also included a postcard publishing company and the popular Delvan's Ice Cream parlor, pictured below, which was once at 307–309 Main Street in Port Washington.

Opposite the Mill Pond on Port Washington's Manhasset Bay waterfront, this building was a bicycle shop and general store in the early 1900s. Run by brothers George and Charles Hyde, this location was also for many years the polling place for old election district No. 3. It later became the Miramar Restaurant, seen in the vintage postcard below. When it was the bicycle shop, it was a very popular business on the waterfront. At that time, bicycling was still a major means of transportation as well as a popular form of recreation. The Hydes' bicycle shop and general store catered to a very lively shoreline as well as to residents who lived around the Mill Pond area adjacent to the bay. William Hyde would later go on to found the *Port Washington News*, which is still in operation.

PORT WASHINGTON AND COW BAY
FROM MILL POND ROAD. ABOUT 1875

For over 100 years, the McKee Brothers General Store stood at the original heart of the Port Washington business community near the Mill Pond. Thought to have been built between 1840 and 1860, the building was first used as a blacksmith shop. Thomas McKee, Port Washington's first postmaster, operated the general store, which made daily grocery deliveries by horse cart. The image below shows the store in its last years in the late 1950s. The land was later acquired by Meadowbrook National Bank in 1959. It is presently the National Bank of North America.

Restauranteur Victor Raimondo and business partner Jack Santomauro acquired 47 Shore Road and named their new seafood restaurant Ship Ashore, capitalizing on the site's location across from Manhasset Bay. From 1984 to 1989, the property saw a succession of owners. In 1989, Raimondo returned as owner with a new vision for the site, one that reflected more of his homeland, Liguria in Italy, than his adopted land of Port Washington. The nautical-themed restaurant was redesigned by local architect Budd Morgensen. Ship Ashore became La Piccola Liguria, and the seafood menu was replaced by northern Italian cuisine. La Piccola secured the devotion of discerning restaurant-goers and gained notoriety beyond Port Washington, establishing a well-known clientele that included actors, politicians, and business leaders. In the early 1990s, La Piccola attracted the attention of Sweden's Stefan Edberg and Bjorn Borg, who dined there while living in Sands Point during the US Open. Upon winning his second US Open title, Edberg held his celebratory dinner at La Piccola. (Both, courtesy of Victor Raimondo.)

After arriving from Germany, Louis Zwerlein opened his Kare Killer barge anchored on Manhasset Bay in 1905. The barge first appealed to the clam diggers and fishermen working on the bay. It prospered until Prohibition forced it to close in 1916. Zwerlein moved the business landside to the docks where Sunset Park is now located; there, he rented out rowboats and sold seafood snacks. Pictured is the business in 1920 with Zwerlein at far left along with his lobstermen and clamdiggers.

One of Port Washington's oldest and most recognizable eateries, Louie's Shore Restaurant ha been a fixture on the waterfront for over 100 years. Originally known as the Kare Killer, it wa a floating barge on Manhasset Bay only accessible by boat during the summer months. In 1916 with the threat of Prohibition, the Kare Killer set up shop adjacent to the Town Dock under the name Louie's (Boats to Let), renting boats and selling seafood. By the 1950s, the business moved to its permanent location at 397 Main Street after it acquired the Horseshoe Restaurant.

Formerly located at 402 Main Street in Port Washington across from Marshall Marine was the Cow Bay Inn, a tavern frequented by the men who worked the shipyards along the bay. A budding art scene during the 1970s led to an influx of art galleries opening up along the bay such as Gallery Odin and the Graphic Eye Gallery, with the latter making its final home at the former inn in 1977.

gallery odin ltd.

322 main street
port washington, new york
516-883-1188

gallery hours
11–5, tues. thru sun.

opening reception ....dec. 14, 3-5 p.m.
show closes ....jan. 31

Opened in 1977 by Betty Gimbel and Annette Fisherman, Gallery Odin Ltd. was located at 322 Main Street in Port Washington. For years, the gallery featured a succession of high profile exhibitions, showcasing prominent art and design of the early 20th century along with contemporary art. Artists such as Alex Katz, Betty Holiday, John Dos Passos, Robert Laurent, Yasuo Kuniyoshi, 1913 Armory Show alumni Wood Gaylor, and many others were represented at the gallery. The spacious, one-floor gallery, with its large windows facing out onto Manhasset Bay, enjoyed several years of success and was repeatedly reviewed in the *New York Times*, *Newsday*, and *ArtNews*. It closed after five and a half years.

Two

Pastimes and Livelihoods

The marshes of Manhasset Bay provide the perfect backdrop for young Lucius Leiber, who grew up amidst a family of recreational boaters. His family moved from Brooklyn to Port Washington in 1903 to enjoy the pleasure of the bay as a break from their prosperous tile business and the crowds of New York City. Launching and building models and toy boats provided hours of entertainment for the young Leiber brothers and cousins, who lived in homes with easy access to the shore and Town Dock. Over two generations, they joined the Knickerbocker Yacht Club, the Manhasset Bay Yacht Club, and the Mill Pond Model Boat Club.

At least three generations can be identified in this photograph taken on Manhasset Bay in the early 1900s. A far cry from the exclusive yacht clubs that populated the shoreline in the 1920s and 1930s, this image suggests the typical weekend outing that broke up the workweek for those whose livelihood, as mechanics, skippers, hunters, clamdiggers, and oystermen, depended on the waters of the bay. This photograph portrays the close-knit family life of a Port Washington

bayman at the turn of the 20th century. As retired harbormaster William Petry observed, "These old baymen were very self-sufficient men. They were hard-working, honest. They worked hard, slept hard, they were in bed 9 o'clock at night and out on the bay before the crack of dawn. And they supported their families. They raised their families."

Waterfowl hunting is a longtime Long Island tradition. Although hunting was originally a way of life and subsistence for families up until the early part of the 20th century, as food became more readily available to purchase in shops, it became less about survival and more about the thrill of the hunt. Duck hunting was an especially popular pastime along Manhasset Bay, with a season that ran from the end of November through January. The above early 1900s image shows two waterfowl hunters at their duck blind, used to conceal the men from unsuspecting ducks. The c. 1900 image at left shows a woman holding the result of a hunting expedition; the caption accompanying the photograph reads, "Preparing for dinner."

Around 1950, legendary Port Washington bayman Tom Kaelin (left) and state game warden Stanley Grom proudly display their catches in Kaelin's handmade duck blind. Kaelin, a life member of the Manhasset Bay Sportsmen's Club and a 50-year member of the Port Washington Volunteer Fire Department, was a renowned expert on Manhasset Bay marine life and waterfowl.

A father and son strategically set their decoy ducks in Manhasset Bay. Hunters would sometime deploy hundreds of decoys to ensure a good spread. As pictured here, the hunter sets his decoy with ample space between them so that they appear to be birds resting in comfort and security

Manhasset Bay was once called the "shellfish garden of New York City," because of its large and plentiful oyster and clam beds. By the 1800s, the area had become the largest oystering harbor on the North Shore of Long Island, yielding thousands of bushels per year. Hundreds of families living along Manhasset Bay supported themselves either by harvesting shellfish or working for businesses that supplied them to the greater metropolitan area. Pictured above are oyster boats tied up to McKee's Dock in Port Washington around 1902. Called skipjacks, these small boats were easily maneuverable in shallow waters and would sail out to the oyster beds daily to dredge for shellfish. Tools such as clam rakes (right) were commonly employed to locate and remove clams from the sediment in the bay. (Right, courtesy of Martha Cooper.)

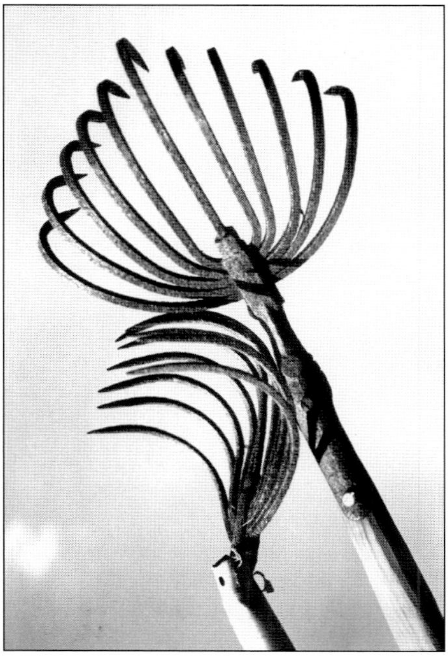

This photograph from around 1900 shows Anie Franke Fraser enjoying her daily sail on Manhasset Bay. She was married to a prominent Port Washington resident, Robert William Fraser, who was a successful fur trader and board chairman at Lampson, Fraser & Huth Inc. Anie shared his love of sailing. An avid boater who also enjoyed fishing on the bay, acquaintances affectionately recounted her often-exaggerated stories of "hooking a sailfish." A proficient sailor in her own right, Anie would often participate in the YRA regattas and special races with her husband, who was the commodore of the Manhasset Bay Yacht Club from 1938 to 1940.

Photographed by Mason Studio photographer Val Gelo in 1960, the Manhasset Bay Sportsmen's Club has brought the age-old ceremony of the Blessing of the Fleet to Long Island waters, a practice going back centuries to early Mediterranean fishing communities. Through its traditional invocation of prayers believed to ensure a safe and plentiful fishing season, the club-sponsored fleet blessings have drawn the maritime community to Manhasset Bay every June since its founding in 1945.

The custom house building, an old waterfront shack located where Main Street runs into Manhasset Bay, stood for many years as a landmark. Originally a rustic hut built to register Long Island Sound cargo into Port Washington, the custom house later became a gathering place.

A meeting place for sailors, yachtsmen, clam and oyster diggers, and fishermen, the custom house was across from the Bradley Hotel as well as the Town Dock after its construction in 1908. The custom house shack was demolished after North Hempstead began an enlargement of the Town Dock in 1949.

John J. Floherty (known as "Captain Jack") was a prolific author from the early to mid-1900s with more than 40 titles to his credit. Floherty was a Port Washington resident for more than 50 years and a member of many local organizations, including the Manhasset Bay Sportsmens Club. It was conjectured that Floherty cofounded the Sportsmens Club while congregating with friends at the custom house.

An informal clubhouse along the shores of Manhasset Bay, The Chicken Point Club was typical of the growing movement to establish recreational clubs in the area. The postcard above from around 1900 is a look back at a landscape that changed drastically with the arrival of the commercial sand mining industry. Once known as Chicken Point, the area between Toms Point and Plum Point in Port Washington is now known as Orchard Beach Once distinguished for its high hills and lush woodlands, the bluffs offered panoramic views overlooking Manhasset Bay onto Great Neck and New York City. Hildegarde Stoeltzing, who came to Port Washington as a child in 1914, recounts her experiences in her personal memoir, "Memories of Chicken Point": "Once in a while we dared to go over to the "Island," now Manhasset Isle. As kids we were sure that there were Indians lurking in the background. But a more idyllic spot cannot be imagined. A wide white beach and just tall trees—a forest of them." Hildegarde's father, Hjalmar Lundin, was a famous prize fighter, wrestler, and "strong man" for Ringling Brothers Circus in 1894. Lundin (below at left) purchased a small summer cottage on Chicken Point sometime around the 1910s where he and his family could enjoy the tranquil waters of the bay. (Left, courtesy of Rose Osterberg.)

As recreational clubs became increasingly prevalent in the early 20th century, acquiring an advantageous location, ideally situated along the shoreline, was essential. Seen here is the Phil Davis homestead, which occupied the plot of land that would eventually be the site of the Port Washington Yacht Club.

Memorial Day is a time when yacht clubs are usually not operating; however, this photograph shows much lively activity along the dock of the Port Washington Yacht Club on its opening day, Memorial Day 1905. Its first home was the former office of the Murray and Reid Sand Company, which excavated sand from the cliffs and hills in the early 1900s. A large sand embankment can be seen in the background.

Pictured here is the Port Washington Yacht Club commissioning ceremony. The ceremony, which celebrates the opening of a new sailing season, relays a series of time-honored rituals among the boating community. The raising of the club's burgee is performed to recognize the founding roots of the club.

This photograph was taken in 1960, six years after a fire in the Port Washington Yacht Club's main clubhouse on January 30, 1954. Club facilities not damaged in the fire included the swimming pool pictured here, the bathhouse, and the pier. Members took the opportunity to organize, and within a year had designed a new, larger clubhouse that could accommodate their growing membership.

Formerly the Cow Bay Skiff Club, renamed in 1910 as the Port Washington Yacht Club, the club moved to its current location in the early 1920s in Port Washington's Bayview Colony. Fifteen years after its formation, the club, now an established and respected institution, held many noteworthy events, including concerts and banquets. In this promotional flyer from 1920, members use humorous wordplay to promote a concert benefit for "disabled and weather-beaten sea dogs."

Founded in 1871 by former *New York Times* editor William L. Alden, the New York Canoe Club, seen here at lower right, is one of the oldest yacht clubs on Long Island, second only to Seawanhaka Corinthian Yacht Club in Oyster Bay. Located on Manhasset Bay's north shore since 1933, it was renamed the North Shore Yacht Club in 1951.

Originally located at the former Americus Club on the Harlem River, the Knickerbocker Yacht Club purchased a plot on Manhasset Bay in Port Washington for a branch station in 1907. The appeal of the bay enticed many club members to make Port Washington their home, and the branch station soon became more popular than the main house in College Point. By 1921, the Manhasset Bay waterfront would become its permanent home after the main clubhouse closed

The intense winter of 1936 motivated members of the Knickerbocker Yacht Club in Port Washington to revive ice boating. Once a popular wintertime activity in the early 1900s, the deep freeze once again presented a frozen bay with ice more than a foot thick. Boats were hauled out from storage and new ones were constructed for a series of competitions every Sunday. The first race of the series included a three-mile course and was open to all, regardless of club affiliation, boat size, or type. The race took place on February 2, 1936, with six boats lined up on the bay. They were Warren Darress's *El Pampero*, Tom Frazer's *Whirlwind*, Jack Aron's *Knickerbocker*, Bob Frazer's *Polar Bear*, Allan Clark's *Feather*, and Gordon Curry's *Papoose*. At just 16 years of age, Darress, who built his own ice boat, took home the silver trophy with 13 points.

Knickerbocker Yacht Club members are pictured with one of their iceboats. On winter weekend when iceboats were raced, the club held open houses where clam chowder was served.

Montague "Monty" Marshall (far left) poses with friends next to his iceboat on a frozen Manhasse Bay around 1930. Louie's Shore Restaurant can be seen in the background. Marshall ran hi family's boatyard and marine supply business, A&R Marshall Inc., which had been founded b his father, Albert, and brother Raymond in the late 1920s.

In the first part of the 20th century, a frozen Manhasset Bay presented opportunities for fun and sport, as evidenced in this undated photograph. Iceboating reached its zenith in the 1930s. In the winter of 1934, the bay froze two feet thick. *Port Washington News* editor Ernie Simon remembered: "Motorists could drive their cars all over the ice on the bay. They would speed up and apply brakes and slide all over the harbor. At night, with headlights on, it was a great sight to see the lights gleaming and moving over the harbor. The temperature stood at 10 below zero for weeks."

Renowned iceboating champion and Port Washington resident Warren Darress typified the yachting community. Darress started iceboating at age 15 and won his first race by 16; he also built his own iceboats. His first boat was constructed from sketches done by his father and incorporated all the fine details associated with true craftsmanship: "I build the boat and all the woodwork, everything, plus make my own runners out of iron. All the metal is cut by hand, and all the hardware. I make my own blocks, sheaves, adjustor devices—all the things that hold the boat together." He is seen here with his iceboat *I-C-Fun*, which he built in 1981.

Frostbiting is the aptly named sport of sailing in a small open boat during the winter months in all types of weather. The sport was rumored to have been conceived in the living room of former Port Washington resident William H. Taylor, yachting editor of the *New York Herald Tribune* and Pulitzer Prize–winning reporter of the 1934 America's Cup race.

World-famous yachtsman Caleb Bragg (left) is pictured with Otto Capra at the wheel of his powerboat *Baby Bootlegger* parked on the ramp of his airplane hangar. Located next door to the Purdy Boat Company shipyard on Port Washington's Manhasset Bay, Bragg's hangar was a local landmark. He was a two-time winner of powerboat racing's most prestigious trophy, the Gold Cup.

Victor Kleisrath (left) of Port Washington Estates and Caleb S. Bragg are shown holding the Gold Cup, which they won numerous times in the 1920s and 1930s. Kleisrath won in 1930 with his boat *Hotsy Totsy*, a Purdy-built boat originally built for Bragg. New York's first Gold Cup regatta was held on Port Washington's Manhasset Bay in 1925. The bay was described by *Motor Boating* as a quintessential location for the 25-race event: "never before has there been a regatta anywhere which has received more advance and complete preparation nor one which in its handling went off more smoothly with almost clocklike precision." Bragg's *Baby Bootlegger* brought home first prize with a speed of 46.43 miles per hour at the 1925 American Power Boat Association Gold Cup Race held by Columbia Yacht Club.

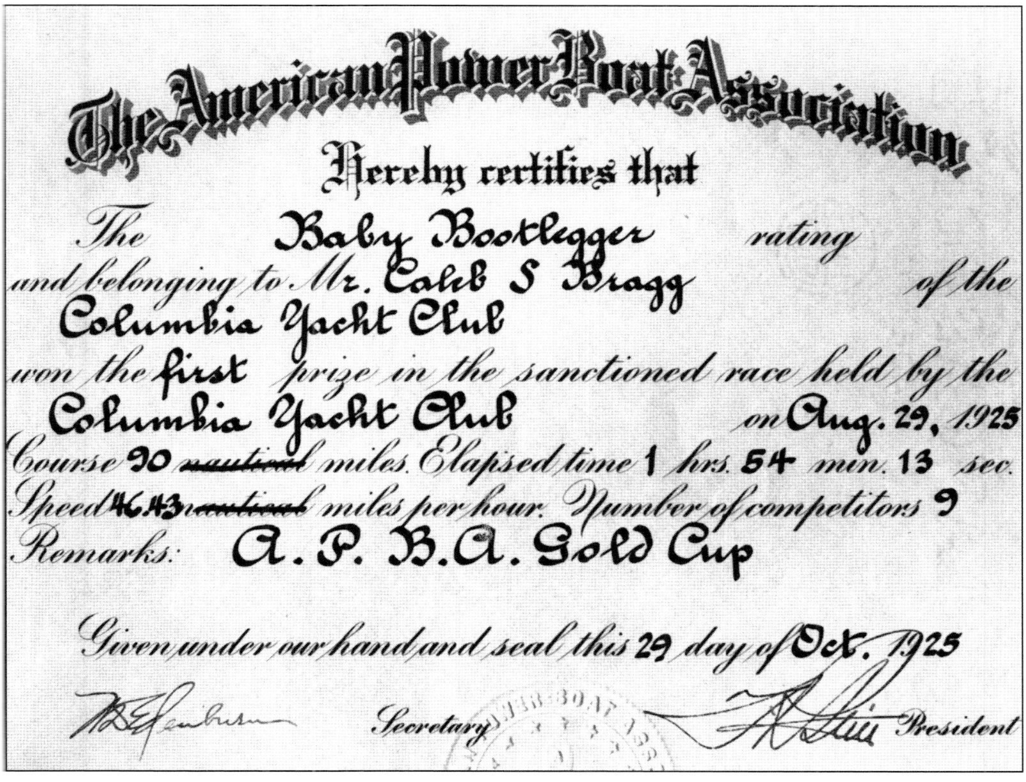

The American Power Boat Association

Hereby certifies that

The Baby Bootlegger rating

and belonging to Mr. Caleb S Bragg of the

Columbia Yacht Club

won the first prize in the sanctioned race held by the

Columbia Yacht Club on Aug. 29, 1925

Course 90 ~~nautical~~ miles. Elapsed time 1 hrs. 54 min. 13 sec.

Speed 46.43 ~~nautical~~ miles per hour. Number of competitors 9

Remarks: A. P. B. A. Gold Cup

Given under our hand and seal this 29 day of Oct. 1925

Secretary President

William Leiber (center) is pictured with one of his hand-built model boats used for racing on Port Washington's Mill Pond, adjoining Manhasset Bay. Leiber was an engineer with Grumman Aircraft Company for 33 years. As a hobbyist, he employed his engineering skills building all types of small working engine models. Leiber's interest in and love for building and racing model boats on Mill Pond started as a youngster and lasted throughout his adult life. In the 1950s, his model boat designs were published in *Model Maker* and *Model Craftsman* magazines.

Stanley Gerard Mason, original proprietor of Mason Studios in Port Washington, photographed many local events, including this swim meet at the Riviera Bath Club on July 17, 1960. The club was part of the Riviera Restaurant at 43 Orchard Beach Boulevard. Built in 1925, it was known originally as the North Hempstead Yacht Club, then as the Columbia Yacht Club. It eventually became the Riviera Restaurant and Beach Club owned by Jack O'Donnell. Famous performers such as Perry Como made appearances there, arriving by boat from the city. The club was destroyed by a fire in 1974.

Considered to be a bathing resort for the Port Washington community, Ed Ryder's Bathing Pavilion provided a quintessential summertime experience in the early 1900s. The pavilion offered bath houses, a tranquil strip of beach for bathing, and light refreshments.

Members of the Reid family, who had lived in Port Washington since the late 1800s, regularly frequented bathing beaches such as Ryder's Bathing Pavilion during the summer months, spending hot summer days along the shores of the bay. Numerous bathing beaches were established along the shoreline in many parts of Port Washington and Great Neck.

Plain Talk

Vol. II, No. 18. PORT WASHINGTON, N. Y., AUGUST 31, 1912 5 Cents Per Copy $1.00 Per Year

COME IN—
THE WATER'S FINE.

Plain Talk was a biweekly publication edited by Henry K. Landis from 1911 to 1914. The magazine discussed Port Washington happenings and community news and included illustrations, advertisements, and poems. Landis, well-versed in the use of glass plate and other photographic techniques, captured in his portraits and landscapes of Port Washington a community in transition from rural to suburban. The recent arrival of the railroad and the attractive waterfront hastened the change. Landis's fervent belief in the importance of public bathing beaches in all communities was expressed in an article in 1912: "A public bathing beach for the use of the entire township, instituted at the town expense would be a wise move while locations are still available. . . . There will be children learning to swim ten years and a generation from now—let us give them the opportunity."

Frances Hodgson Burnett (1849–1924) was a famed author and playwright, best known for her classic children's novels *Little Lord Fauntleroy*, *A Little Princess*, and *The Secret Garden*. Although Burnett led a transatlantic life, in 1907, she permanently relocated to the United States and, in 1911, built Fairseat, a grand estate in Plandome Manor overlooking Manhasset Bay (above). Burnett loved to spend time in the expansive gardens on the property, which were evocative of the eponymous garden in her novel *The Secret Garden*. The house was nicknamed "the Archways" after the arches placed along the walks on the grounds—an elderly Burnett is pictured at left standing underneath one such arch. (Both, courtesy of the History Center at the Manhasset Public Library.)

Alphonse Henry Alker (1851–1912) was a prominent New York attorney, real estate investor, and co-founder/vice president of the Pennsylvania Cement Company. An enthusiastic yachtsman, Alker built a grand estate, Idlewilde, on Manhasset Bay in Great Neck in 1896 to better enjoy the pristine waters of the bay. Alker and his family would stay at Idlewilde during the summer, entertaining guests and spending time on Alker's steam yacht *Florence*. The image below shows two boaters in Alkers Cove, the area of Manhasset Bay adjacent to the Idlewilde estate. (Above, courtesy of Alice Kasten; below, courtesy of the Great Neck Public Library.)

Chartered in 1925, The Port Washington Lions Club is one of the oldest Lions Clubs on Long Island and one of the first service clubs in the community. The civic-minded club has been instrumental in raising awareness of and providing funding for projects and organizations for cancer research, Industrial Home for the Blind, Heart Fund, Salvation Army, St. Francis Hospital and North Shore Hospital. Locally, the club created and developed Lions Field, a 12-acre athletic complex for Port Washington youth activities. Following a season of service to the community, club members would usually partake in a recreational boat ride. Pictured above are club members boarding the *Ilse III* on Manhasset Bay about to set sail for a boat tour of Manhattan. Below, a more intimate group of members has lunch on a tugboat cruising through the bay, bound for Long Island Sound, in the summer of 1929. The tugboat, which was also used to tow sand barges, belonged to Lions member Fred Grauweller. Seated on the deck from left to right are Dr. Arthur Gilette, Dick Townsend, Leo Ryan, and Burt Monfort.

A Port Washington mainstay from the 1920s through the 1980s, the Sands Point Bath and Country Club (below) provided all the amenities of a classic country club. During the summer, it served as a family getaway offering pools, tennis courts, and access to the adjacent beach along Manhasset Bay in Sands Point. Black-tie dinners and dances attracted the social elite. Jack Miller, who lived in Sands Point in the 1930s, wrote the words and music for "Sands Point is Nearer to Heaven" around 1939. Before this, he was for many years the arranger for Kate Smith, a radio and recording singing star. From its initial debut at the Sands Point Bath and Country Club, the song became an instant hit, quickly becoming a popular part of the club's weekend events. The sheet music cover at right, designed by Frank Daniel, was reprinted and offered as a 75th anniversary souvenir in 1985.

Manhasset Bay Yacht Club (MBYC), seen in the background of this photograph, was an outgrowth of the Douglaston Yacht Club. It moved to Port Washington in 1891 and is still an active part of the community today after more than 120 years. As it enjoys a prime waterfront location, the yacht club is a great place to go swimming during the summer, as evidenced by this image of bathers posing on the club docks before taking the plunge.

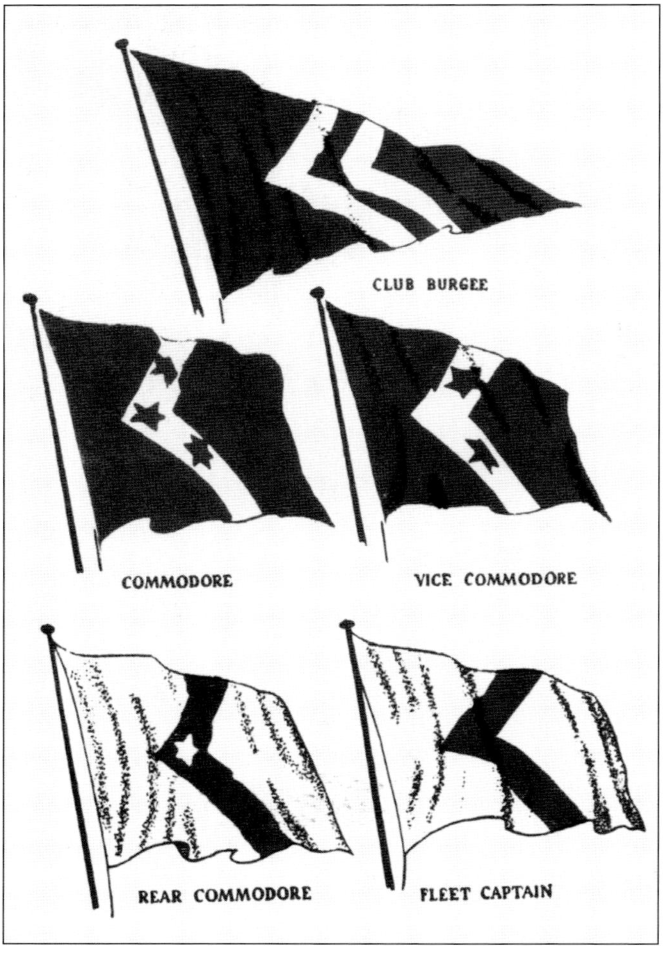

Flags were an important communication tool between ships at sea and on land. Burgees were designed to identify recreational boating organizations. This page from the 1963 Manhasset Bay Yacht Club yearbook shows the club's burgee along with officers' flags.

The American eel is found in streams, rivers, estuaries, and marine waters on the eastern coast of North America. Once common in Manhasset Bay, eels were an important catch for the Matinecock Native American tribe, and later, the white settlers of the area. The fish had use both as food and as bait to catch other creatures. This late 1800s–early 1900s image shows fisherman Tom Townsend skinning the eels caught during a day's fishing expedition on Manhasset Bay.

Once dubbed the "dean of Port Washington lobstermen," Tom Kaelin's life as a bayman spanned nearly three quarters of a century. A lobsterman, eel trapper, clam and oyster digger, and fisherman, he was a highly respected waterfront fixture up until his death in 1988. A highly decorated lifetime member of the Manhasset Bay Sportsmen's Club, Kaelin has received numerous awards for his expertise, including the coveted Dannenfelser Award in 1958 as well as earning the title Bayman Emeritus from his time as Port Washington's bay constable in the 1950s. Pictured is Kaelin with his boat loaded with lobster pots at the Town Dock around the 1970s. After building his lobster pots, Kaelin would often use a small propane tank to brand them so that they would be easily recognized when collecting. (Courtesy of Ted Cronyn.)

This August playbill from the Hunters Town Dock Theatre was from the inaugural season that began June 26, 1956, and ran for 10 weeks in the summer. The concept emerged in 1955 when husband and wife thespians Philip and Ruth Hunter rented the large storage shed at A&R Marshall's Marina which was vacant during the summer when boats covered the bay. In addition to performance space they included the Green Art Gallery, and artists contributed a portion of their proceeds to fund a children's clinic in Pusan, Korea. The theater showcased performing groups including the Little Club of Manhasset, the Port Washington Play Troupe, and the East Coast Studios of Warner Brothers.

Manorhaven's shorefront park famous for its pool, first opened to the public in May 1964 and is the centerpiece of a series of recreational areas, especially after its 2011 renovation. The swimming pool (added in 1964) was modified several times, most recently creating a 25,000-square-foot pool with two waterslides, lap lanes, kiddie pool, water play area, and a 12,000-square-foot bathhouse with space for events and food service. Above, two excited children pose outside the pool's entrance on its dedication day. The photograph below, taken several months later in July 1964, shows a crowd enjoying the newly opened pool.

With the picturesque Manhasset Bay as its backdrop, Manorhaven Beach Park and Pool is a popular and scenic recreational locale. This aerial photograph shows its expansive grounds. In the early 1900s, the area was known as Locust Grove, and before that, it was a rural area where chickens and cows were raised along the water's edge in an area called Orchard Beach (an area roughly from Tom's Point to Plum Point). A pond once existed where the ball field in Manorhaven Beach Park is now located. (Another pond was across the road, which was Chicken Point Road, now Manorhaven Boulevard.) A section of land along Manorhaven Boulevard and the bay, called Chicken Point, made up of wetlands was filled to create the park area, which roughly consists of 34 acres with 300 feet of beachfront. An impressive range of amenities includes athletic fields for baseball, softball, soccer, tennis, basketball, racquetball, and bocce courts; horseshoe pits; a boat ramp; and playgrounds.

Three

SHIP SHAPE SHORELINE

A steam yacht, sailboat, and cruiser meet in the middle of Manhasset Bay in the 1920s. It was not unusual for members of the various yacht clubs and maritime workers to get together and shoot the breeze on a calm day on the bay. Many skippers lived on the streets that dead-ended on the bay, so their civic duties, families, and seafaring duties overlapped. From a working harbor to "a sailor's paradise," the waters of the bay were a focal point for the town's commerce and transportation as well as its leisure activities.

The *Masquerader*, pictured above on Manhasset Bay, was an 85-foot, comfortably appointed cruising yacht owned by world-famous yachtsman Caleb Smith Bragg. It was captained for 10 years by Peter Petersen, known for his reliability, as stated by Braggs in a 1931 letter of recommendation: "We have cruised from Newport R.I. to the Florida Keys, without a single accident, in fact I have never had a single claim against the insurance Companies. I feel this is quite a record for a boat that has been in commission every year, and an equally good record for the Captain." Pictured below are the crew of the *Masquerader* around 1930, with Captain Petersen at far right. Bragg sold the yacht shortly after. Petersen would later be employed by O'Brien Brothers, who then owned the largest sand and gravel company on the eastern seaboard.

In the spring of 1909, Albert R. Marshall opened a shipyard at 403 Main Street in Port Washington. Known as A&R Marshall, it soon became a thriving business—hauling, storing, repairing, and servicing more than 150 ships a season. Marshall also performed yacht fittings and sold marine supplies, boats, and engines out of his machine shop, the interior of which is pictured above around the early 1900s. A&R Marshall was eventually known as one of the largest and best-equipped marine service shops on Long Island and retained its name even after it was sold in the early 1970s. Boats stored at Marshall's for the winter, and the launch ramp that would return the boats to the water in spring, can be seen below around 1950.

Monte Marshall designed and built this speedboat when he was 22 years old. In the background is the future site of Sunset Park with the old police station to the left. Marshall is fueling his boat at the Socony gas station's pump across from the Town Dock.

Louis J. Larsen Inc. was founded by Larsen, a native of Denmark, in the early 1900s. The company was originally located in Manhattan at 45 Fulton Street and later at 50 Warren Street. In the early years, Larsen made sails for commercial vessels. As commercial sailing vessels began to disappear, the business turned to producing sails for racing, cruising, and day-sailing boats. He and his wife, Hilma, had two sons: William and Louis A. After Larsen died in 1959, the company was later run by his son Louis, who relocated to 40 Matinecock Avenue in Manorhaven. The company was sold to Doyle Sailmakers in 1988.

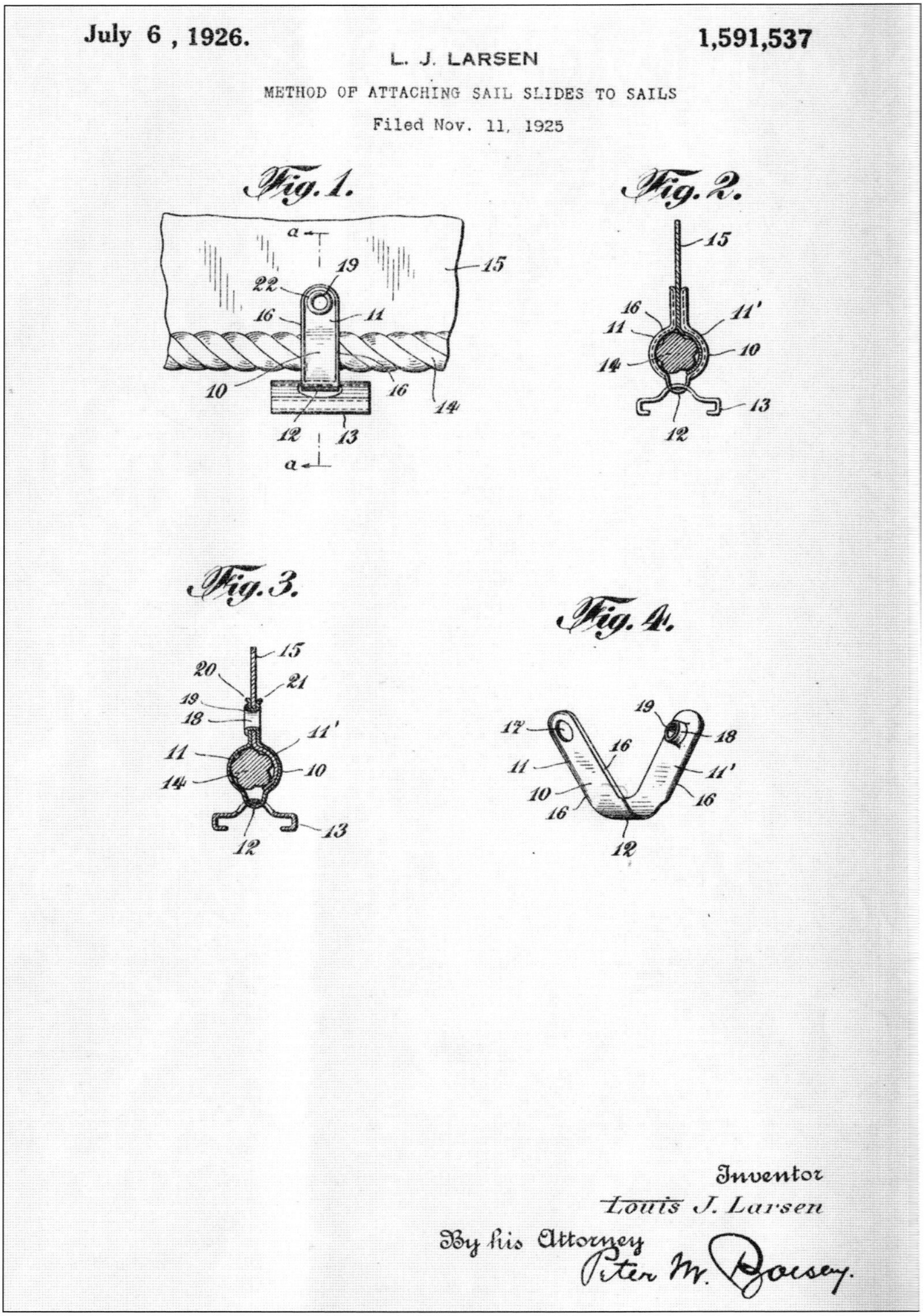

Larsen's proclivity for sailmaking led him to experiment with more functional methods in constructing sails. He submitted numerous applications to patent his designs, as shown in this drawing for a patent from 1925 for attaching sail slides to sails.

Above, boatbuilder Donald White (left) is pictured with Mikey Kulich, boatyard owner, as they work on *Angelita III*. It was custom designed by Gerald White, formerly of Westlawn Associates in 1963, as a sedan cruiser with a V bottom and raised deck. White used oak, fir, and mahogany in its construction. The *Angelita III* was eventually gifted by New York businessman Arthur G. Gossner to the Aquacultural Engineering Laboratory in Wareham, Massachusetts, a branch of the University of Massachusetts, as a research vessel. (Courtesy of Donald White.)

First built for John Hay Whitney in the late 1920s, the *Aphrodite* underwent a complete redesign by Purdy after its initial design (not designed by Purdy) did not meet expected high-speed standards. Whitney commissioned the Purdy Boat Company to build the 74-foot yacht in 1936. Moored at the Port Washington Yacht Club, the legendary *Aphrodite* was also used for entertaining celebrities and by Pres. Franklin Delano Roosevelt for military service. In an oral history conducted in 199 Budd Mogensen, whose father helped build the Purdy *Aphrodite*, recounted the intricacies of the boat's specialized design: "I believe that a lot of other people didn't want to build that boat. Too tricky. At that time you gave guarantees. You know this boat will go 'x' knots an hour for so long and use so much gasoline. And if you don't make it you don't get paid." Above is the initial construction for the *Aphrodite* at the Purdy Boatyard, and below is the *Aphrodite* on Manhasset Bay. (Above, courtesy of Alan Dinn.)

In the c. 1925 photograph above of the original shop building in Port Washington are Purdy workers posed in front of what is surmised to be Carl Fisher's Gold Cup racer *Baby Shadow,* Port Washington's first Purdy-built boat. The interior scene of the Purdy engine shop below shows mechanics working on a Packard Gold Cup engine for race-boat owner George Reis. From left to right in the foreground are Reis, Anderson Bowers (Reis's mechanic), Bob Purdy (engine shop manager), unidentified, and Art Purdy. (Both, courtesy of Alan Dinn.)

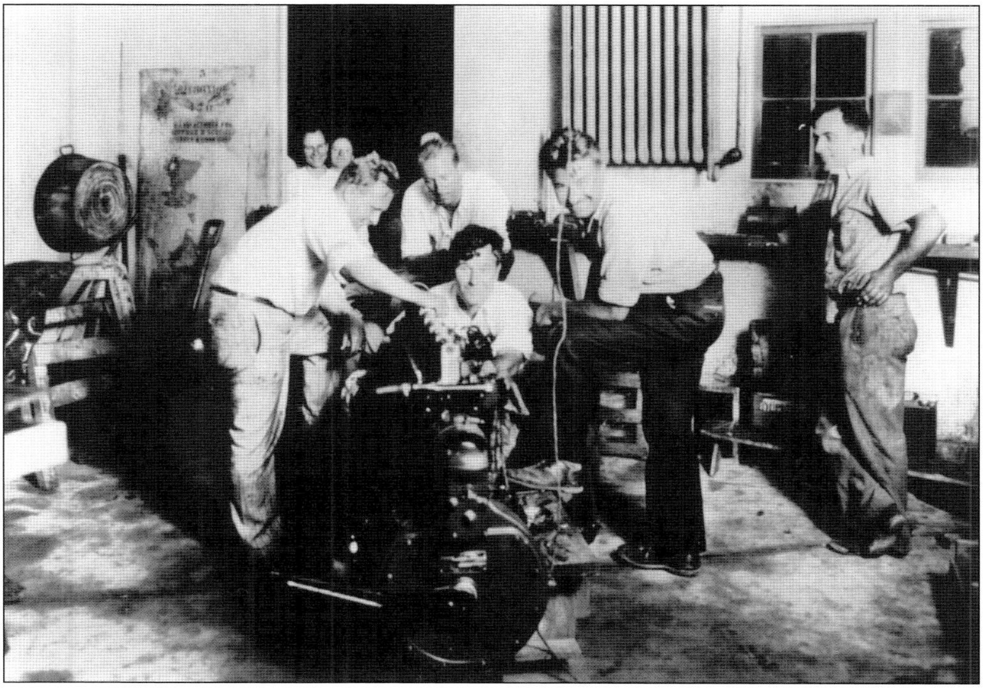

This scene of the Purdy shop in the mid-1930s shows a production line of Star-class racing sloops The Great Depression nearly wiped out the firm and left its clients with less cash to spend on custom yachts and racing boats. Starting in 1931, however, orders for Stars began to come into the shop, and as Purdy quality became known, many well-known sailors began to order more boats Over time, the Purdys built 34 of these boats. The Star had a long connection with Manhasset Bay—the design was inspired by Commodore "Pop" Corry of the Manhasset Bay Yacht Club, and the first Stars were built at the old Isaac "Ike" Smith yard in the winter of 1910–1911. (Courtesy of Alan Dinn.)

Most of Ike Smith's early career was spent building oyster sloops and various other crafts for the local fishing industry in Port Washington. In the early 1900s, he was commissioned by local yachtsmen to produce 11 Manhasset Bay Bug-class racing yachts designed by the office of William Gardener. By 1910, he built the first 22 Star boats, and by 1928 had completed 80 of them as one of four partners in the Sands Point Boatyard along with several more by 1930. Smith retired to a relatively quiet life of building rowboats in the backyard of his Port Washington home, which he built himself in 1912.

Purdy Shipyard built several wartime military vessels, including 20 picket boats in 1943. These boats were small, quick, and relatively inexpensive to build. They were constructed by Purdy through war bonds sold by the First Federal Savings and Loan Association. The funds were raised by individual areas in the community that then named and launched their own boats. Among them were *Miss Port Washington*, *Miss Baxter Estates*, and *Miss Port Washington Heights*. *Spirit of Harbor Acres* (seen here) was christened by Jane Priscilla Albert, granddaughter of John Phillip Sousa, and launched on September 11, 1943, from the docks at the Purdy Shipyard off Bayview Colony in Manhasset Bay. Vigorous campaigns, rallies, and other promotions were used to encourage war-bond purchases in communities. In Port Washington, fire departments carried war bond banners on their trucks in the annual Memorial Day parade, and the Port Washington War Bond Committee hosted theatrical events at the Beacon Theatre on Main Street.

In August 1941, the USS *Augusta* is seen anchored at the entrance to Manhasset Bay on its way to the Brooklyn Navy Yard for repairs and alterations. The ship was returning through Long Island Sound from Narragansett Bay, Rhode Island. Its purpose was a clandestine meeting between two of the most powerful world leaders of the time: Pres. Franklin D. Roosevelt and Prime Minister Winston Churchill. The result was a joint declaration, the Atlantic Charter, which included eight common principles that outlined Allied goals for the war, a framework for peace and cooperation among nations, and a commitment to work for disarmament in the postwar world. The private dock in the foreground was part of the Alexander and Elisabeth Lewyt estate near the mouth of Manhasset Bay.

The MS *Schwabenland*, a German ship out of Bremen, is seen above moored in Manhasset Bay in Port Washington sometime around 1936. It was first launched as the *Schwarzenfels* in 1925 for transport between Bremen and India. It was purchased in 1934 by the German airline Deutsche Luft Hansa (now Lufthansa) and renamed *Schwabenland*. In September 1936, the ship was stationed in the North Atlantic and launched catapult airplanes (pictured below) as part of Germany's worldwide airmail system. (Both, courtesy of the Walter Christensen Collection.)

Walter Christensen, a former Pan American employee at the Port Washington facility, documented through his photography the aviation advancements happening at that time on Manhasset Isle and Manhasset Bay. Christensen is pictured with his wife, Elsie, aboard the MS *Schwabenland*. (Courtesy of the Walter Christensen Collection.)

Virginia "Ginger" Marshall Martus (1930–2017) was born in Port Washington in an era rich in maritime culture. The heir to a renowned boat building enterprise, she was the daughter of Raymond Marshall, co-owner of A&R Marshall Boatyard and Marine Hardware in Port Washington. Pictured here is Ginger, age seven, at the wheel of a small boat with her sister Claire and grandmother on Manhasset Bay around 1937. Ginger grew to become an expert on nautical history, writing numerous publications on the subject. A former historian and lifetime member of the Port Washington Yacht Club, she also helped found the Nautical Advisory Committee at the Port Washington Public Library, a committee still active today.

Edmund B. Carns was an innovator and developed many sheet metal and airplane patents. His interlocking steel canoe showcases Carns's prowess in metal design. These images, taken by former Mason Studios photographer Stanley Gerard Mason in the 1940s, display the Carns design brought to life. Carns used a version of his last name for his company, Cairns Sheet Metal, which was located on Yennicock Avenue in Port Washington. Its last known year of operation was 1948.

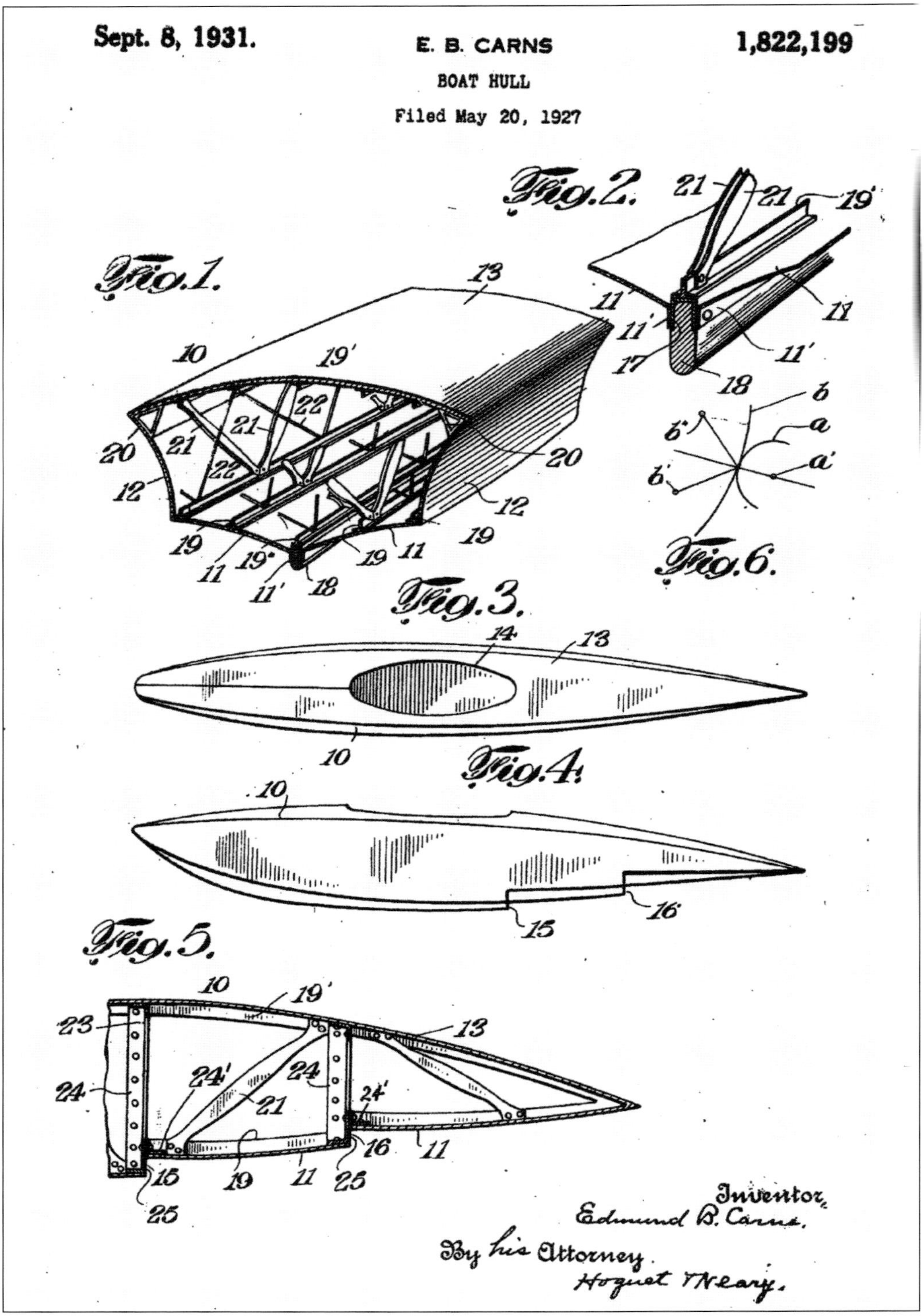

Edmund B. Carns was listed in the 1930 Index to Patents as the assignor for the Cairns Development Company of Wilmington, Delaware. Carns created several sheet-metal patents, including this 1927 patent design for a boat hull.

One of the last surviving examples of its type, the *Benjamin Packard*, a once grandiose 244-foot square-rigged sailing ship, is shown here anchored in Manhasset Bay off Wampage Shores, a development in Plum Point. At this time, the *Packard* had already gone through a succession of owners and even had a brief stint as a US Merchant Marine training vessel. It was orphaned in Manhasset Bay after its previous owner, Theodore Roosevelt Pell, had the ship towed from Newtown Creek. Pell, a once-prominent real estate developer in the area, was credited with developing the Plum Point area into Wampage Shores in the early 1900s.

Houseboats, or "float houses," as they are sometimes called, are boats that have been designed to be used primarily as a home. Although most are capable of operating under their own power, they often remain stationary, staying moored close to land to provide shelter and utilities. Houseboating is appealing to many due to the ability to explore the local scenery, remain in close proximity to other outdoor activities, and the potential to move for a change of view on a whim. Manhasset Bay, with its safe anchorage and beautiful harbor, became an ideal location for houseboaters starting in the 1940s. A houseboat is pictured here around 1945.

Although some people exclusively use houseboats recreationally during the warmer months, others choose to live on these floating homes permanently. Former Port Washington dock master Jim Flemings lived year-round on his houseboat, the *Home Sea Home*, at the Riviera Marina where he worked until 1975. Manufactured by Holly Park, the fully insulated craft is pictured here in October 1970. (Courtesy of Jim Flemings.)

The 33-foot sedan cruiser *Adair II* was designed by Eldredge-McInnis and built for Kenneth W. Meytrott of Manhasset by the Peterson Shipyard at 451 Main Street in Port Washington. The *Adair II* was supplied with a pair of Chrysler Crown engines with two-to-one reduction gears and had a top speed of 20 miles per hour. Its home port was the Port Washington Yacht Club. The cruiser is pictured above around 1948 just off Sands Point. The Peterson Shipyard was one of several on the shores of Manhasset Bay.

The Manhasset Bay Marina is located in a sheltered section of Manhasset Bay near Tom's Point. The 300-slip facility has been owned and operated by the La Motta family since the early 1980s and includes an onsite waterfront eatery, La Motta's Waterside Restaurant, where sailors and landlubbers alike can eat a meal while enjoying a view of the bay. The marina also sports a full-service yard where boat engines and hulls are repaired. This c. 1990 image shows a shipyard worker glazing the bottom of a boat to protect it from the harsh marine environment.

In order to bring essential fuel to the Port Washington shoreline during the cold winter months Lewis Oil tugs broke through the ice when Manhasset Bay froze over. These tugs also used sand mining companies for winter transport, often breaking through ice 12–14 inches thick. The tugs met large supply boats out at the mouth of the bay to guarantee that fuel would always be available at their docks on Shore Road. A small water lane, overseen by Capt. Edward Lewis would be kept open for the supply boats arriving from distant points, enabling the distribution of fuel, coal, and oil to the Lewis Company.

Virginia Marshall Martus took this photograph of Larry Waring driving his tugboat *Emerald City* on Manhasset Bay around 1985. Designed and built by Waring at Marshall's Marine, the tug was exclusively used for family trips and leisure boating. Draped on the bow are the signature handmade "puddings" of Waring's wife, Jan.

Four

INDUSTRY

Workers construct Port Washington's Town Dock on Manhasset Bay around 1909. While there was some debate as to where the dock should be located, it has been conjectured that the final site was credited to Charles F. Lewis, one of Port Washington's first postmasters. Lewis would later become the second county treasurer of Nassau County.

For more than four generations beginning in the early 19th century, members of the Cocks famil[y] were actively involved in the daily commercial and political life of Port Washington and Nort[h] Hempstead, residing mostly in the village of Port Washington North. Various branches of th[e] family owned and ran gristmills that provided grain for local households. They also held politic[al] office and served as firefighters, farmers, sand miners, contractors, postmasters, businessmen, an[d] major landowners along the shore road that paralleled Manhasset Bay. Seen here is the five-stor[y] Cocks Grist Mill constructed in 1781 by Adam Mott on Shore Road near the former site of th[e] Lewis Oil Company.

In 1687, William Nicoll, son of early English settler Matthias Nicoll, the sixth mayor of New York from 1672 to 1673, inherited his father's 600-acre homestead in Plandome. After acquiring an additional 400 acres, he commissioned Joseph Latham to build a tidewater gristmill on Manhasset Bay in 1693 near Gildersleeve's Creek (later Mitchell's Pond, now Leeds Pond). After the property was sold to Latham in 1718, the manor house and mill were passed down through generations of Cow Neck families including Latham, Mitchell, Hewlett, and Leeds. The main structure, with minor alterations, still stands today as a private home. The mill was moved 120 feet from North Plandome Road to its present site. Because the structure maintained some of its original elements, including beams and millworks, it received historic recognition from the Cow Neck Peninsula Historical Society's Historic Designation Plaque Program.

Located near Orchard Beach Boulevard in Manorhaven, Ben Morgan's Old Ferry Dock was heavily used when regular ferry service ran on Long Island Sound and the adjacent Manhasset Bay. Once the Triborough Bridge and Whitestone Bridge opened in 1936 and 1939, respectively, ferry services ceased operation. The old ferry dock has since been refurbished. In the summer of 2019, through efforts by the Village of Manorhaven, the dock reopened to the public as Morgan's Dock Park.

American entrepreneur Carl Fisher, who developed Port Washington's Bayview Colony in the 1920s, built this home on Manhasset Bay. Regarded as a visionary, Fisher's biggest success was his development of Miami Beach when it was nothing more than a mangrove swamp. He had planned to do the same for Montauk in the 1920s, during which time he kept an office in Port Washington. In 1929, the stock market crash dashed his dreams of creating a "Miami of the North" on Long Island.

New Versailles on Manhasset Bay was a development project proposed by the National Academy of Design in the 1920s. The construction was to be "an expression of the highest in art and the most exclusive in human environment," situated on some 200 acres on Manhasset Bay. The intention of New Versailles was to offer the art-lovers of America an opportunity to live in a community that defined modern artistic expression. New Versailles proclaimed the United States, which had emerged from World War I a world power, ready to "take its rightful place in the world of art." It was to be composed of two groups of chateau-like residences, a clubhouse, restaurants, and stores surrounded by beautiful gardens and lagoons inspired by the Palace of Versailles in France. The proposed location on the North Shore of Long Island was most desirable for its proximity to New York City as well as the aviation fields of Garden City, the races at Belmont, and the waters of the bay. Captured in this illustration is the opulence envisioned by the planners of this grand project for the edge of Manhasset Bay. Fortunately for the character of the North Shore, it never became reality. (Courtesy of the History Center at the Manhasset Public Library.)

Guarding the entrance to Port Washington, Toms Point (right tip of Manhasset Isle, in the foreground) shows the way to Town Dock (left). The grid marks for future streets in the soon-to-be developed Manhasset Isle in Manorhaven can be seen in this 1927 aerial photograph.

A sign at the intersection of Manhasset Avenue and Shore Road lists new homes for sale on Manhasset Isle around 1948. Capitalizing on Manhasset Isle's waterfront allure, developers (such as Callahan) would run weekly advertisements to entice new home buyers with the "reasonable prices," "beautiful sandy beaches," and "shore dinner specialty . . . right at your door."

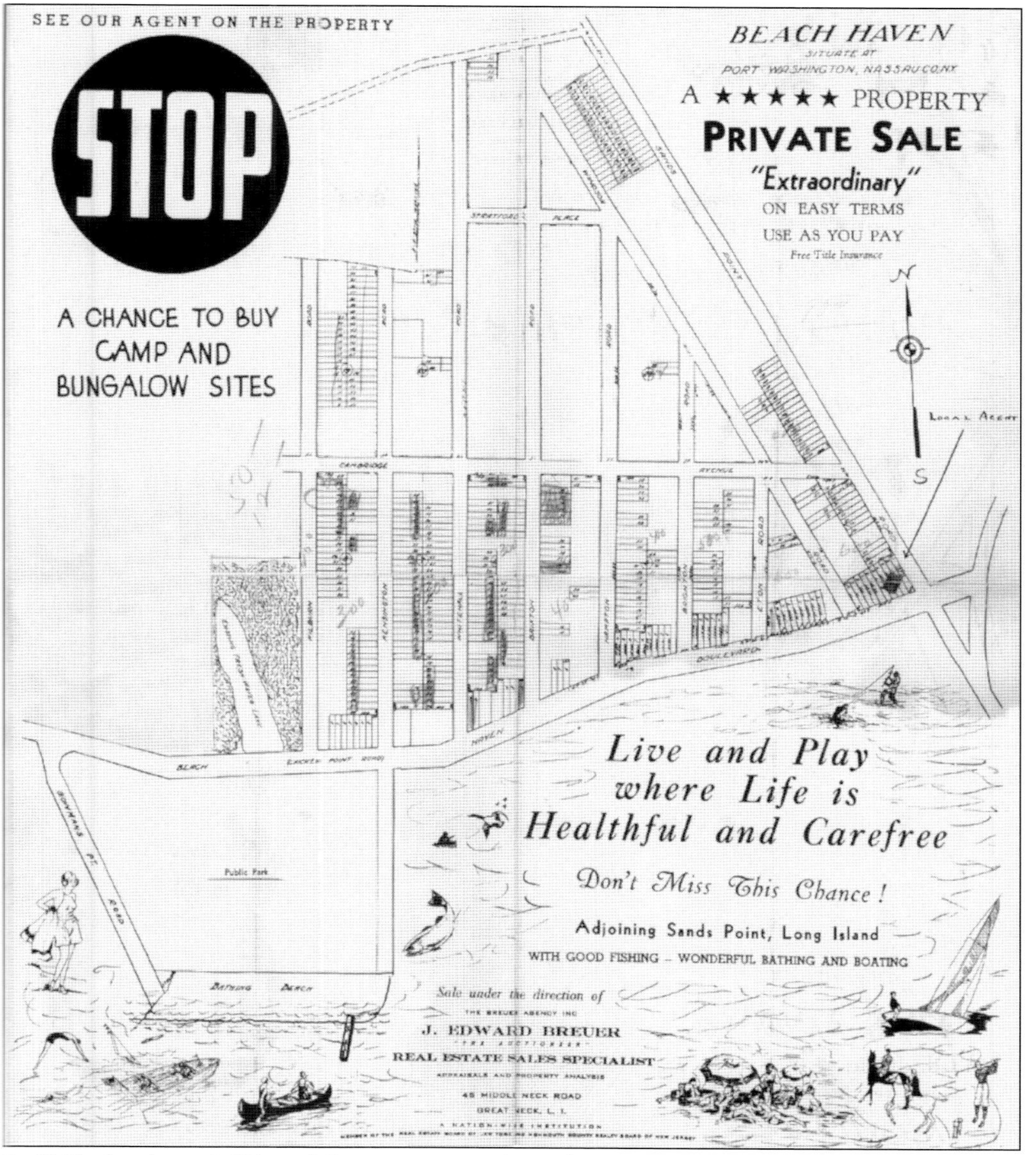

In 1938, developer J. Edward Breuer, owner of a real estate agency in Great Neck, New York, predicted one of the largest home purchase seasons since 1927 was about to occur and noted in particular the high interest in summer homes on Manhasset Bay: "Never before has the summer bungalow been placed on a par with all other real estate." His advertisement for a large bungalow community, Beach Haven, included a significant portion of the village of Manorhaven—eight blocks along Manorhaven Boulevard (labeled Beach Haven Boulevard) from Sands Point Road to what would become Hickory Road (labeled Kilburn Road) and bordered by the village of Sands Point. Oddly, Breuer's street names recalled tony sections in the city of London and not a casual bungalow community in Port Washington, New York. Breuer's plan never came to fruition. The bungalows built were on streets named Boxwood, Cottonwood, Dunwood, and so forth. The community became a seaside resort after World War II for many Italians looking for sun, sand, recreation, and time away from their Brooklyn and Bronx communities; in time, their weekend bungalows became their permanent residences. (Courtesy of Alicia McCarvill.)

The Copp Brothers Realty Company, operated by brothers Wesley and Albert Copp, along with Thomas Gorman, developed much of the area in Manorhaven, once known as Orchard Beach. The brothers' father was C.W. Copp, a prosperous lumber merchant from Flushing, Queens, who first sought to develop this area in the 1920s by advertising small plots he had acquired for bungalows

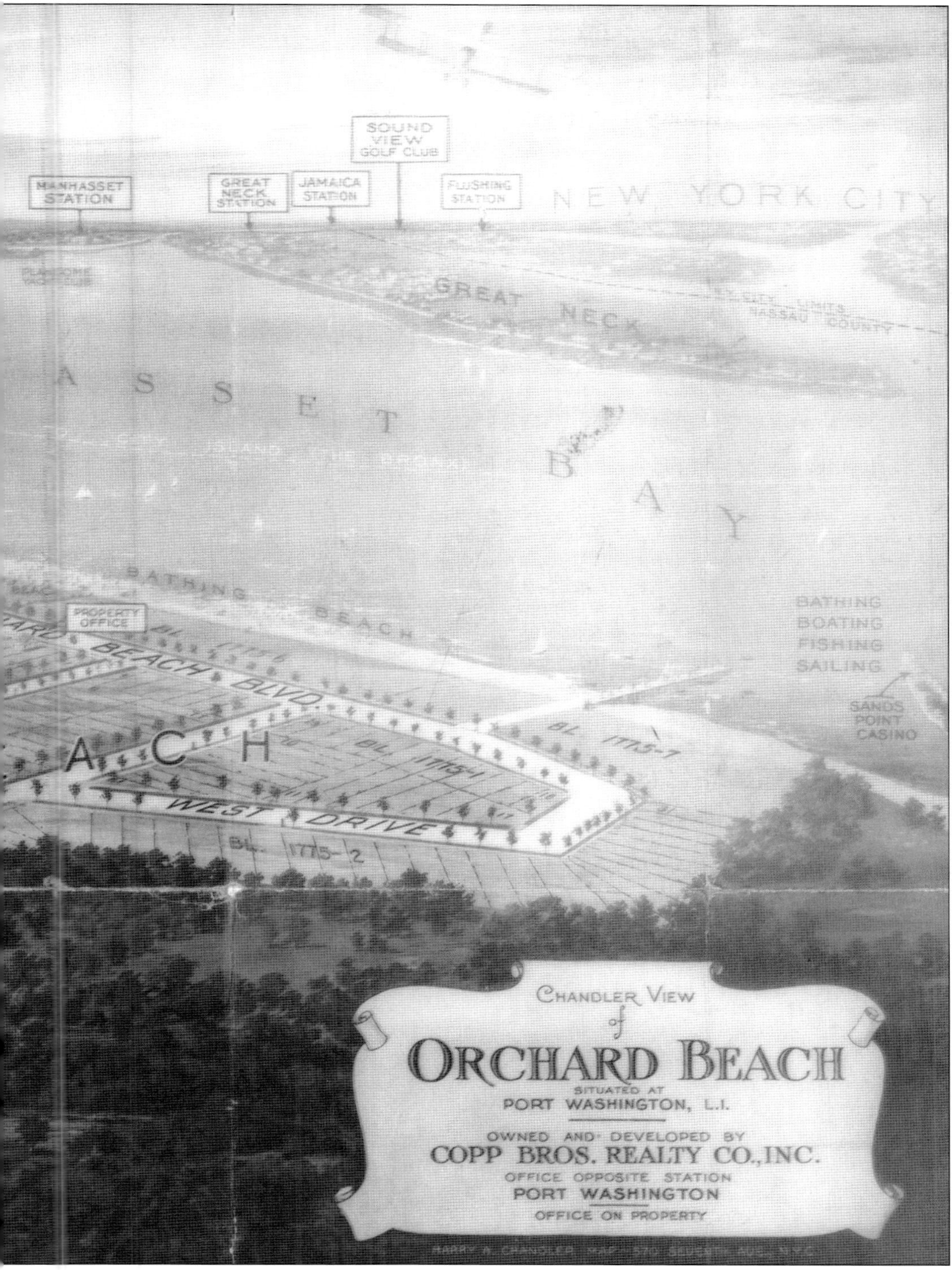

When stringent zoning laws were adopted by the Town of North Hempstead, Copp formed his own village in an attempt to evade new codes that would interfere with his development. The village of Manorhaven in Port Washington included Orchard Beach, Beach Haven, and Manhasset Isle. Wesley Copp became the village's first mayor when it was incorporated in 1930. (Courtesy of Jim Flemmings.)

Proximity to Manhasset Bay attracted big businesses such as sand mining companies Goodwin & Gallagher and the Lewis Oil Company. In this aerial photograph from around 1950, the Lewis Oil facility—offices, storage tanks, and piers for their tugs—is at center. Surrounding the Lewis facility is a complex rail system that conveyed sand from the mined cliffs across Shore Road on conveyor belts to waiting barges lining sections of Sheets Creek. Today, the landscape of barren sand and oil storage tanks along Shore Road is dominated by two shopping centers, the Soundview Marketplace and Delco Plaza, and behind them lie residential subdivisions. (Courtesy of the Village of Port Washington North.)

Above, a fleet of Lewis Oil trucks is lined up alongside oil tanks on Shore Road in 1936. Founded before the turn of the 20th century as a shellfishing venture, the company began with the Lewis family transporting their harvest of clams and oysters to Manhattan's Fulton Fish Market. They turned next to transporting coal as demand for the fuel increased for heating the homes of residents along Shore Road and the Port Washington peninsula. Once coal became the central product, the name changed to the Lewis Coal Company. When the family noticed the growing popularity of oil, which outpaced coal as the primary fuel for heating, the name changed again, to Lewis Oil Company. Below, workers construct oil storage facilities at the company's tank farm on Shore Road around 1945; the structures were completed about 1950.

The flattened peninsula of Manhasset Isle, stripped to its sandy base by sand mining operations in the early 1920s, offered opportunities for a new industry. Pictured under construction in 1928 is American Aeronautical Corporation's factory and flight station on Manhasset Bay in Port Washington. The company purchased 16 acres in February 1929 and planned a massive 235,000-square-foot facility for building Savoia Marchetti seaplanes, a school, and a seaplane terminal.

The Type S-55 from Port Washington-based American Aeronautical Corporation was also known as the Savoia-Marchetti S.55 flying boat. Introduced in 1927, it was the first monoplane with twin hulls and side-by-side pilot's cockpits and achieved fame on long-distance flights. Tandem engines were carried on struts on the top of the aircraft. Seen just below it in the background is the Socony gasoline station and gas barge on the bay around 1929. (Courtesy of Court Commercial Photo Inc.)

Capt. Charles Blair, a pioneer of transatlantic aviation and former chief pilot for Pan American World Airways, founded Antilles Air Boats Inc. in 1963. Using a Navy surplus Grumman "Goose" seaplane, Blair foresaw the potential for passenger traffic in the Caribbean. Pictured is one of Blair's Antilles Air Boats in Manhasset Bay around 1965. In 1979, the airline was acquired by Resorts International through the approval of the Civil Aeronautics Board when Blair's wife, Hollywood actress Maureen O'Hara, was the airline's president and chief executive officer.

In 1977, Capt. Charles Blair made a second excursion by flying boat across the Atlantic Ocean. Taking off from Port Washington's Manhasset Isle, Blair flew a World War II vintage flying boat to Lake Derg, Ireland. Seen here is the actress Maureen O'Hara (who was married to Blair at the time) arriving by boat to the Manhasset Isle hangar. O'Hara was one of 16 passengers on the flight, including J.C. Kelly, former pilot to Winston Churchill.

On September 6, 1922, aeronautical pioneer Glenn H. Curtiss managed to make a nine-second sustained flight with his 140-pound aquatic glider, or "sailplane," on Manhasset Bay. This accomplishment came as somewhat of a surprise, as it was achieved only after four unsuccessful attempts and occurred while the plane was being towed into position by a speed boat. A slight breeze that had been absent earlier in the day blew over the bay, making it possible for Curtiss to release the tow rope and glide without motive power of any kind. This event was termed "the first step in sea soaring" and marked the beginning of aquatic gliders. Pictured here, the Curtiss Model 29 SX4-1 rests on a dock before its pivotal launch on September 6, 1922; Curtiss is at center in a suit and cap. (Courtesy of the Glenn H. Curtiss Museum, Hammondsport, New York.)

Pictured is the flight crew of the first TWA flight from Port Washington to South Africa in 1946. Capt. Hugh Herman stands to the left and chairman of the board T.B. Wilson is on the right. The flight included a full crew with one purser, three pilots, one flight engineer, one radio operator, one navigator, and one flight hostess, Dorothy Darress (center). Darress (nee Beck), who first worked for TWA as a teletype operator and passenger agent during World War II, was selected and trained by the airline to become a flight hostess. She was expected not only to look the part, maintaining certain physical requirements such as weight, but was also expected to be well versed in geography and cloud formation. She was the first TWA stewardess to cross the Atlantic 100 times and the first to log one million flight miles. This was her inaugural flight as a TWA stewardess.

In 1909, Goodwin Sand & Gravel, a successful sand mining company, requested the town of North Hempstead permanently close Sands Point Road so that it could continue its mining operations from sections of what would become the village of Manorhaven up to the edge of the village of Sands Point, including the sand supporting the road and beyond into what would become the school district property for Sousa Elementary School and into the village of Port Washington North. The request, while originally approved by the highway commissioners and the town board, was vehemently opposed by several Sands Point landowners, who challenged the decision in court and won. In 1910, an agreement was reached by both parties that enabled Goodwin to construct a tunnel under Sands Point Road connecting its operations. For nearly 10 years, the company used cars pulled by a small steam engine to move sand under the road to waiting barges in Manhasset Bay. Pictured here is the entryway at the end of the Sousa Elementary School parking lot adjacent to Sands Point Road.

Albert Marino, the son of a sand miner, worked for almost his entire professional life in some aspect of the sand mining industry in Port Washington. Marino is pictured overseeing the loading of Port Washington–mined sand onto barges destined for New York City construction projects. Sand from the area came from a number of shoreline mines, several of which Marino worked for on both sides of the peninsula. In an interview for the Port Washington Public Library in 1981, Marino said, once "all the mountains and the hills were all there and if you look at it today they're not there. But I think that's part of working in the sandbank. The land goes."

Five

From Battered to Beautiful

Manhasset Bay, one of many harbors along the Long Island coast, was hit hard by the 1938 hurricane. Considered at that time to have been one of the strongest storms to strike the East Coast, storm surges inundated the bay, smashing many boats of all sizes against the docks. Powerful winds brought heavy damage to structures along the shoreline. Longstanding shore businesses such as the Port Washington Yacht Club received devastating damage.

From the porch of Gaffney's Seafood Restaurant, once located near the Town Dock, Port Washington residents could do little to delay the devastation of the 1938 hurricane, only observing the residual damages caused by wind gusts over 129 mph.

This was the back storage yard at A&R Marshall Shipyard at high tide after the 1944 hurricane. Land is underneath the crane in the distance, and the Knickerbocker Yacht Club dock (seen at far left) is completely submerged under the water.

First conceived by Gay Pearsall in 1962 as a permanent concert hall, the Sousa Band Shell outdoor performance space was built to honor composer and musical conductor John Philip Sousa, who lived in Port Washington's Sands Point from 1915 to 1932.

Pictured is the Sousa Band Shell ribbon-cutting ceremony in 1967. From left to right are Gay Pearsall, Sol Wachtler, Helen Sousa Albert, Nassau County executive Eugene Nickerson, and unidentified. The name Sunset Park was chosen because of the westerly exposure across the bay, giving a clear view of beautiful sunsets. The park's name was suggested by George Wallingford.

Port Washington photographer Rene Reeves was inspired by Port Washington's aviation histor to capture several images of the abandoned and decrepit Republic Aviation Corporation site mor than 20 years after its closure and subsequent abandonment in 1965. The land, which was onc home to other big names in aviation such as American Aeronautical and Pan Am, was later sol to Thypin Steel, a steel storage company, which owned it until the late 1980s. The building sa vacant for more than 20 years, a neglected waterfront fixture.

In 1968, a small group of Port Washington residents concerned with the loss of open space an proposed high-density expansion in their community formed Residents for a More Beautiful Por Washington, which evolved into an environmental advocacy organization now named Resident Forward. In its nearly 40-year history, it has been recognized as a leader on the town, county state, and national levels. Members of the organization, seen here around 2001, continue thei efforts for beautification near the Mill Pond and along Manhasset Bay.

Remnants of abandoned boats, stacks of debris and decayed wood, and leftovers from the harbor's industrial past are visible in this image of a neglected and degraded Sheets Creek. An offshoot of Manhasset Bay, Sheets Creek is bounded by Manorhaven's Manhasset Isle and Port Washington North. In the late 1990s, a radical initiative to eradicate Sheets Creek of pollutants was launched. Efforts were made by the Waterfront Advisory Commission, the Town of North Hempstead, the Village of Manorhaven, and local marina owners, resulting in more than 20 tons of debris being removed from the water.

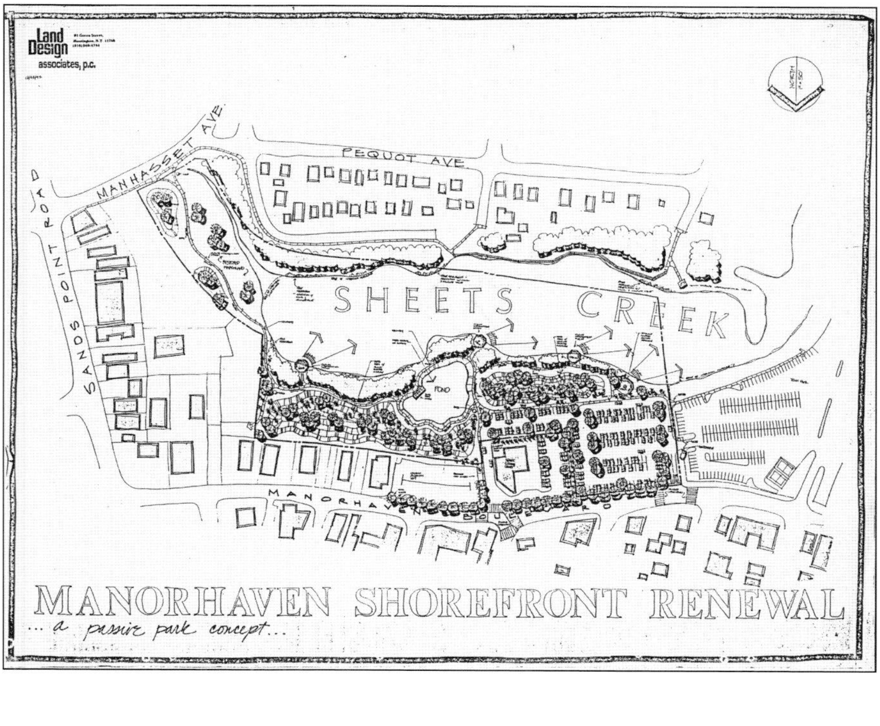

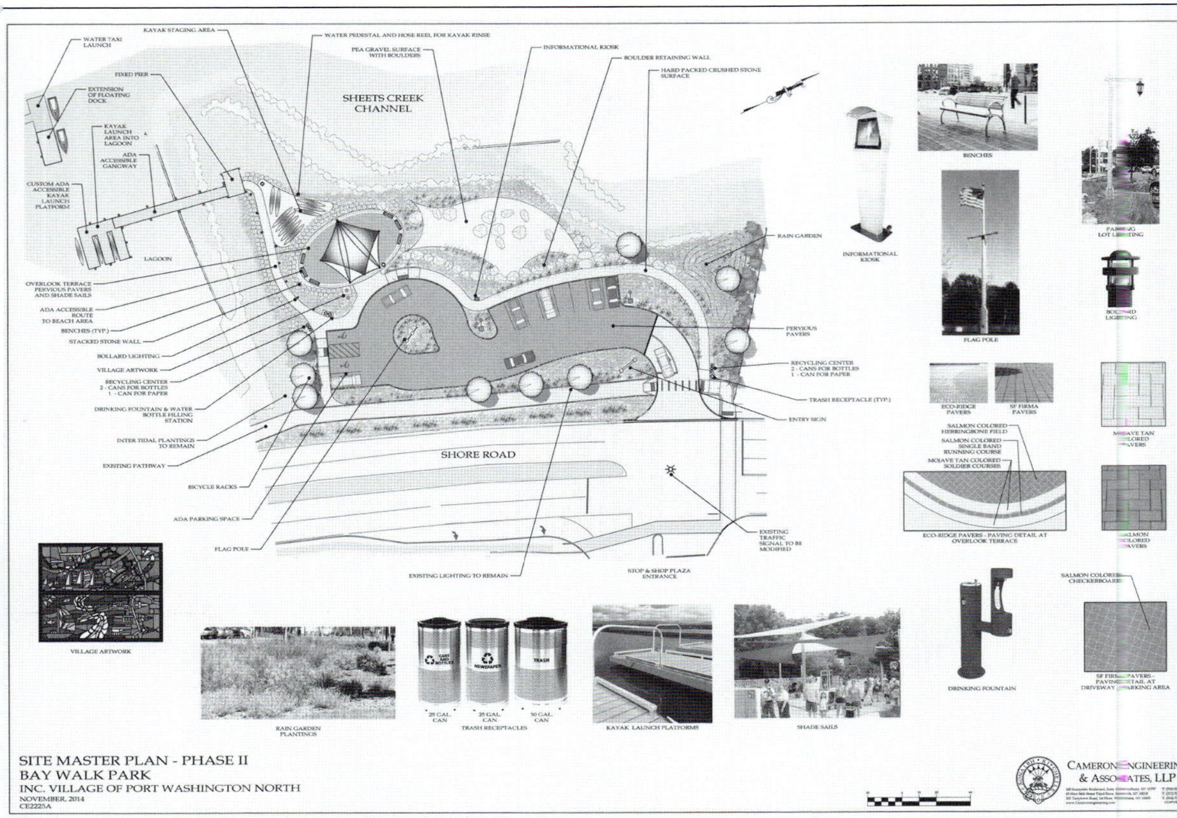

The Port Washington North Bay Walk Park Project, an ambitious community project 13 years in the making, is one of the crowning jewels of a reinvigorated waterfront. Neglected waterfront property, mostly utilized for industrial purposes, destroyed the natural beauty of the shoreline that borders Manhasset Bay and Sheets Creek to the west. Over a decade, the Village of Port North turned the area into an active waterfront park, encouraging outdoor activities such as walking, cycling, kayaking, and nature watching. (Courtesy of Bob Weitzner.)

Six

ART OF THE BAY

Plein air, creating natural scenes outside the confines of the studio, has always been customary along Manhasset Bay and is still practiced by many North Shore artists. This image from around 1900 shows a seated artist at right preparing to sketch a morning seascape.

The presence of a variety of watercraft in the harbor inspired local model makers such as John Lindroth to recreate scenes in miniature. A licensed master and first-class deepwater pilot for 36 years, Captain Lindroth lived a block away from the shore of Manhasset Bay in Port Washington. After retiring in the 1960s, he used his basement workshop to craft wooden models of boats and people he knew during his working years. His artistry was featured in articles in the *New York Times* and *Motor Boating* magazine. Lindroth's workshop was filled with hand-cut model boats, wheels, carving tools, and miniatures. The miniature model of the J-class yacht *Ranger* below includes the figures of Commodore Vanderbilt at the wheel and sailor Arthur Knapp to his right.

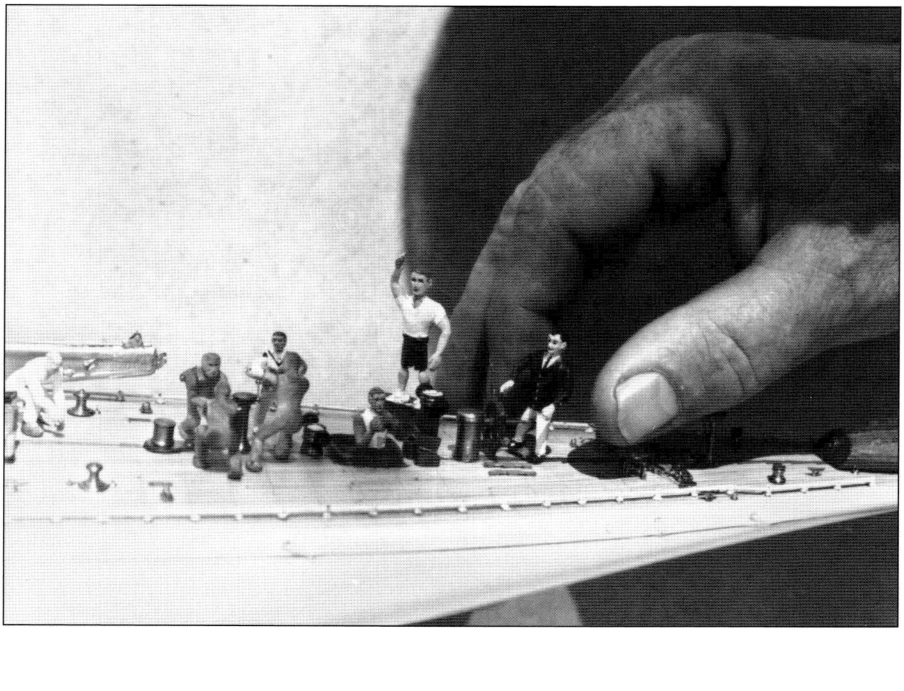

John Lindroth, who crafted custom-made ship wheels in the 1960s and 1970s well into his 70s, worked in his home workshop at 35 Second Avenue in Port Washington for 30 years near the Manhasset Bay waterfront. After retiring in 1963, Lindroth devoted himself to making both functional and decorative ship wheels utilizing teak for outdoor applications and ebony and ash for indoors. Pictured here is a Lindroth wheel turned into a coffee table. (Courtesy of Dave McKeever.)

Tugboats were an important presence on the Manhasset Bay shoreline since the early decades of the 20th century. They were used to push and pull barges heavily loaded with sand to their final destinations. An oral history interview conducted by the Port Washington Public Library in 2007 captured memories of the Trap Rock plant. Sand miner and artist Dan McCann and coworkers James McCann and Robert Langone recalled the docks, the dangers, and the deliveries of sand and gravel to New York City during their 40 years of work. McCann, who created this watercolor and many others, shared his fascination with and experiences on Manhasset Bay.

Bow puddings, or protective fenders, like other traditional maritime crafts once linked to the working harbor, are now part of a recreational culture. Once a typical sight on tugboats and other commercial vessels, the practice has become a lost art form. Local Port Washington resident Jan Waring first learned to make puddings (also known as "mushes," "baggywrinkles," or "fenders") from Eddie Mallon, a former tugboat captain for the Lewis Oil Company. Waring, seen here working on one of her hand-made puddings at the Manhasset Bay Marina in 1992, would tightly weave a hemp-like rope around a synthetic core that would not rot. (Courtesy of Martha Cooper.)

Rigger David James hails from a family of sailors. As a young man, he started rigging sailboats, employing traditional tools and techniques handed down from earlier generations of sailmakers and riggers. Like those before him, James used tools and techniques of masters such as Al Larsen and Jack Liddell, who had to adapt to the changing landscape of their trade. James would often use techniques such as wire splicing and fancy rope work in his constructions. (Courtesy of Martha Cooper.)

Model boat maker Mario Tribuno of Port Washington, seen here in his workshop, often created his models working directly from the original. Striving to always create works that were significant to his own life, he often incorporated wood from historic structures gifted to him by his fellow Manhasset Bay Yacht Club members. At left, Tribuno employs a woodworking technique known as chip-carving. Using a knife, he removes small chips of wood from a flat surface in a single piece. (Both, courtesy of Mitch Carucci.)

Cecil Akre, a longtime Port Washington resident who lived in a house with a full view of Manhasset Bay, was an avid sailor and member of the Manhasset Bay Yacht Club. Born in 1925, he served in the Navy in 1942 and, before earning a law degree, worked on commercial shipping vessels going between South America and the United States. Despite the demands of a busy career, Akre's artistry in waterfowl carving earned ribbons at exhibitions in Maryland and on Long Island. Akre, seen at right in his workshop, created the yellow-leg decorative decoy below, which was featured in the 1993 Port Washington Library exhibition Changing Channels.

Port Washington resident Jim Wood learned about nature firsthand as a child while fishing, boating, and swimming in Manhasset Bay and Long Island Sound. Later in his life, as a professional artist and award winning decoy carver, Wood began collecting historic decoys as a source of inspiration for his own creations. Carving gulls, wood ducks, blue bills, and fish, Wood took pride in creating his own unique patterns, doing his own research and "carving 'em as I see 'em." (Both, courtesy of Mitch Carucci.)

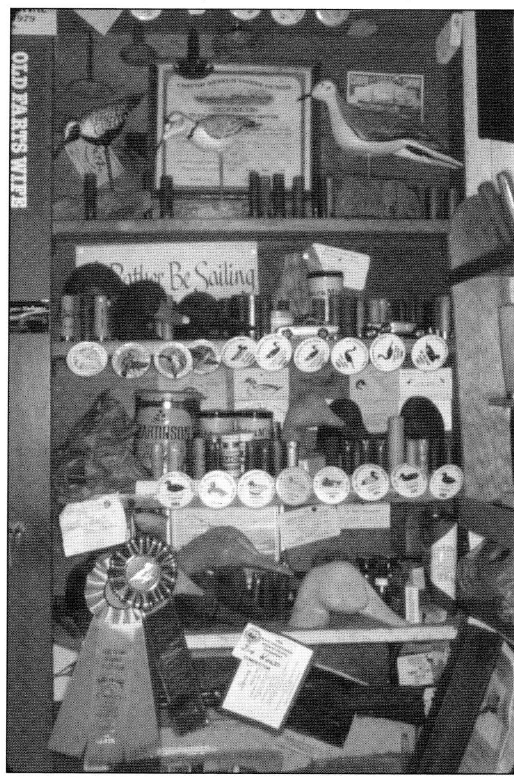

"When people look at the Bay, they see a duck. When I look at the bay, I see blue bills, mallards, black ducks, old squaw, merganser, geese, brants," said John Salerno in an oral history interview in 1992 at the Port Washington Public Library. As a model maker, Salerno is a craftsman whose work reflects years of living by the bay. His painted wooden decoy ducks recall morning duck hunts and the sight of dozens of duck blinds spread out between Port Washington and Great Neck. Descended from the old local oystermen and clam diggers who gathered at "city hall" (near the Town Dock), Salerno continues the tradition of decoy carving and taxidermy he learned from his father and uncle.

Samuel Cocks, who was born deaf, painted scenes of his surroundings. He was a clammer, and his family owned the five-story tidal gristmill that is depicted here. Using twigs, stones, sand, and grasses collected from the nearby beach, Cocks created an evocative diorama with the mill pond in the foreground and Manhasset Bay in the background. The mill was demolished in 1910. The Cocks family were a distinguished family, bound to the land and water associated with local clamdiggers who had a major influence on the development of this community.

William Galloway was a Port Washington police officer from 1929 to 1946 and later became police commissioner. However, his passion was capturing picturesque Port Washington scenery in art, particularly the surrounding Manhasset Bay area. Galloway's trademark whimsical and highly detailed style is perfectly represented in this 1962 pen and ink drawing of Bradley's Restaurant. This is one of several local businesses and nautical scenes Galloway depicted.

Locust Grove, formerly situated along the Manhasset Bay shoreline by what is now Orchard Beach Boulevard, was a very popular summertime retreat in the early 1900s. At that time, excursion boats traveling from New York City would make regularly scheduled stops at the Grove during the summer, as depicted in this rendering by artist Bill Galloway from 1962.

This large wall hanging was created in 1974 on the 100th anniversary of the Knickerbocker Yacht Club, on the shores of Manhasset Bay. Along with the Port Washington Yacht Club, the North Shore Yacht Club, and the Manhasset Bay Yacht Club, the Knickerbocker attracted members who enjoyed ice boating, racing, and sailing on the protected waters of the bay. This artistic rendition of its history includes the club burgee and images of the yachts and sailboats captained by such racing luminaries as Emil "Bus" Mosbacher and Edward du Moulin. The clubhouse, shown at lower right, was demolished in 2012 to make way for the Knickerbocker Hotel and Condos at the same location on Port Washington's Main Street. Having survived two world wars, the Great Depression, and major hurricanes, the club could not sustain its membership numbers and closed in 2007. What remains are memories of its glory days and continuing legacy of the internationally renowned Knickerbocker Cup.

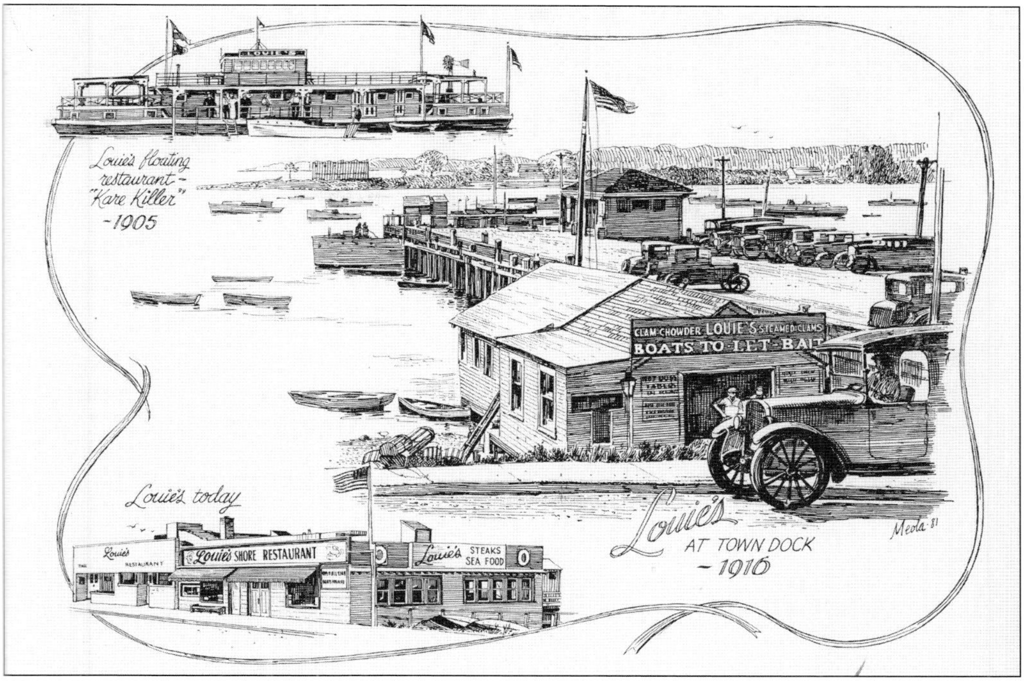

This 1981 promotional place mat design depicts the various iterations of Louie's Restaurant over the many years it has been in business. From its early beginning as a rough-hewn restaurant barge through its reinvention as a boat rental and chowder house, to its expansion and modernized interior and exterior of today, this pictorial depiction perfectly portrays its colorful history through the ownership of four generations of Port Washington's Zwerlein family.

Prominent Long Island artist Charles Henry Miller (1842–1922), an original member of the Manhasset Bay Sportsmens Club, painted this scene of the Town Dock in Port Washington around the 1920s. Known primarily for his landscapes and etchings, Miller sought to capture the fishing-club vibe found on the dock where members of the Sportsmens Club first met.

Mary Olmstead Johnson (1890–1950) began painting in the early 20th century. Focused on capturing the quotidian life of the people around her, Johnson's subjects included life around Manhasset Bay. In this watercolor scene titled *Manhasset Bay Boats Dry-Docked at Low Tide*, Johnson depicts the local Port Washington fishermen waiting for their next fishing tour along the bay. (Courtesy of Bill Ciccariello.)

A longtime resident of Port Washington, Ann Scrofani Pellaton (1921–2018) lived her entire life within sight of Manhasset Bay, an influential element in many of her works. This watercolor from around 1980 is indicative of her style at that time. Pellaton was the president of the National Association of Women Artists and a founding member of the Graphic Eye Gallery, Long Island's longest-operating art gallery cooperative. (Courtesy of R. John Pellaton.)

The Graphic Eye Gallery, formerly located at 402 Main Street in Port Washington, was the longest running cooperative art gallery on Long Island. Founded in 1974, it was established by a group of local female artists while at the studio of Aida Whedon. A Port Washington printmaker and teacher, Whedon also ran an art school with her husband, Dan. Offering a creative space for artists to meet and exhibit their work, the Graphic Eye's goal was to form a gallery for artists managed by artists. It changed locations several times before finally settling near Manhasset Bay until it closed in 2018. (Courtesy of R. John Pellaton.)

Iconic Port Washington artist and instructor Aida Whedon (1915–1994), at center, sought to create a collaborative network of local women artists who would learn printmaking and create artwork in her studio on Bayview Avenue in Port Washington. These women brought with them their own expertise and unique styles. Several of these artists would exhibit at the Graphic Eye Gallery. Surrounding Whedon clockwise from left are Ann Pellaton, Betty Gimbel, Catchi Childs, Barbara E. Fishman, and Marion Klein.